The Best of
INDONESIAN COOKING

The Best of
INDONESIAN
COOKING

Yasa Boga

TIMES EDITIONS

© 1998 Times Editions Pte Ltd

Published by Times Editions Pte Ltd

Times Centre
1 New Industrial Road
Singapore 536196
Fax: (65) 2854871 Tel: (65) 2848844
E-mail: te@corp.tpl.com.sg

Times Subang
Lot 46, Subang Hi-Tech Industrial Park
Batu Tiga, 40000 Shah Alam
Selangor Darul Ehsan, Malaysia
Fax & Tel: (603) 7363517

Printed by Toppan Printing Co. (S) Pte Ltd

ISBN 981 204 043 9

CONTENTS

Preface

Yasa Boga means 'food maker' in Indonesian, and *The Best of Indonesian Cooking* is based on our years of personal experience as four homemakers who are, at the same time, career women.

This book is targeted at the uninitiated as it is filled with practical information to ease them into the world of Indonesian cooking. We have sections on Indonesian cooking equipment, the various herbs, spices and seasonings commonly used in Indonesian cuisine, and the variety of fruits, buds and leaves that can be transformed into succulent and delectable dishes. Also included are tips on where these basic ingredients can be found and what to use as substitutes if they are not available.

This compilation contains recipes from all over Indonesia. Packed with a tantalising range, from spicy curries and grilled chicken to exciting fried noodles and exotic salads, it is guaranteed to entice the blandest of taste buds!

We have included the places of origin for nearly all the recipes so that readers may familiarise themselves with the different cooking techniques used throughout Indonesia. Also included are bits of information about the lifestyle and culture of Indonesians.

All the recipes in this book are easy to follow; the measurements are exact and the steps are well-described—making them simple to reproduce and guaranteed to be mouthwatering!

Yasa Boga
1998

Indonesian Kitchen Equipment

~

Contrary to popular belief, preparing Indonesian food is rather simple. You need only a frying pan or a wok, a few sizes of pans, a steamer, a griller, a spice and seasoning grinder and a coconut grater. This chapter will give you a better understanding of Indonesian kitchen equipment.

FRYING PAN OR WOK

A frying pan or wok is used to fry, sauté or cook a curry. The size of utensil used depends on the quantity of ingredients called for in the recipe. We recommend possessing at least one 30 cm frying pan in which to fry a 500 gram fish.

There are several types of pans to choose from: aluminium, cast-iron, stainless steel, enamelled or teflon-coated. Avoid using a cast-iron or aluminium frying pan or wok if a dish contains acidic ingredients because acid dissolved at high temperatures in such utensils will ruin the natural colour of the dish.

UTENSILS FOR FRYING

A wok scoop is used for stirring and turning over food while a perforated ladle is used for lifting deep-fried food and draining excess oil.

You can also use tongs to turn over deep-fried food.

PANS

Heavy-bottomed pans are used to cook rice so that the rice does not get overcooked.

STEAMER

A steamer can be used to cook rice and other dishes through the evaporation process. Steaming can be done in a wok using a bamboo or aluminium steamer. The steamer is placed inside a wok just above the level of boiling water and is covered during cooking.

Pans

Steamer

Grilling wire

Grill with base

Wok scoop and perforated ladles

Woks with metal sieve

Tongs

Steel skewers

Blender

Rice cooker

Steamer

Grinder

Grater

Saucer-shaped grinding
stone with pestle

Mortar & Pestle

GRILLING OVER A STOVE

A grilling wire is made up of two pieces of wire which can be separated and clamped together. The food is clamped between the wires, and is placed over the fire. The grilling wire is turned over frequently so that the food is cooked evenly.

A grill with a base is also made up of two pieces: the grilling wire and the base. The base is heated when grilling food. Since the food is placed on the wire above the base, it will not be in direct contact with the flame.

GRILLING IN AN OVEN

Use the heat from the heating element on the upper part of the oven. When grilling satay, use steel skewers because they do not burn nor break easily.

GRINDER FOR SPICES

There are several types of implements for grinding spices:

A saucer-shaped grinding stone with pestle, sometimes made of clay.

An oval-shaped grinding stone with pestle, which is easier to use since both hands can be used to grind.

A deep mortar with pestle.

A food processor which usually consists of two parts: the blender for blending spices into a wet paste, and the grinder for grinding dry spices or nuts.

GRATER OR JAGGED-EDGED
SPOON (Kukuran)

The grater is made of wood or iron.

A jagged-edged spoon (kukuran) is used to grate coconut flesh. The grated coconut flesh is then squeezed to extract coconut milk. This equipment is widely used in Sumatra, Malaysia and Sri Lanka.

The simplest way to obtain coconut milk is to blend coconut flesh and water in a blender. Grind until very fine. Then strain the liquid through a sieve and squeeze the flesh to extract the coconut milk.

RICE COOKER

A rice cooker can be used to cook rice with coconut milk. Cook 250 grams washed raw rice and 350 cc water over medium heat. When the water is almost absorbed, add 100 cc thick coconut milk and all the necessary spices.

Basic Ingredients

~

In this book, you will find recipes from all over Indonesia. Almost all the recipes require basic ingredients that are commonly found in Indonesia. Fortunately, most of these ingredients can also be bought at Asian food stores in many big cities. Look out also for advertisements in food magazines for mail-order catalogues that specialise in Asian herbs, spices and other foodstuffs.

COCONUT

Mature coconut: its skin is brownish black, and it has a high oil content. It is suitable for use in oily dishes such as *rendang* (beef in coconut milk).

Half-mature coconut has yellowish skin and contains a lot of milk. Not as oily as mature coconut, it is preferred for curries such as *lodeh* (vegetables in coconut milk), *opor* (chicken in coconut milk), or for making traditional cakes.

Young coconut has light brown skin and tender flesh, and does not contain much milk. Young grated coconut is used for *urap* (vegetables in spiced grated coconut) or *botok* (salted fish in coconut milk).

Very young coconut has skin and flesh too soft to be grated. It is usually used for making drinks or as a traditional cake filling.

Poyah/ambu-ambu is grated flesh from a mature coconut that has been roasted and ground until the oil seeps out. If no fresh coconuts are available, use desiccated coconut as a substitute.

Coconut water from mature, half-mature and young coconut will add a reddish tinge to *gudeg* (young jackfruit in coconut milk) and a sweet taste to fried chicken and *tempe bacam* (fermented soybean soaked in coconut water).

COCONUT MILK

This white and delicious liquid is produced by mixing grated coconut flesh with water and squeezing it to extract the juice.

Mature coconut

Half-mature coconut

Coconut water

Poyah / ambu-ambu

Coconut milk

Instant coconut cream

Coconut powder

Young coconut

Very young coconut

Grated coconut

Desiccated coconut

Palm sugar

Green chillies

Bird's eye chillies

Garlic

Onion

Brown sugar

Dried chillies

Shallots

Red chillies

Curly red chillies

Frozen grated coconut can last for about 30 days. Put fresh grated coconut in a plastic bag and keep in a freezer. Before using it, add hot water in order to get coconut milk of a good quality.

If you are using fresh coconuts for cooking, it is best to peel off the brown skin. This will help to retain the natural colour of your dish and prevent it from turning black. For oily dishes, choose a mature coconut with the skin intact.

If no fresh coconuts are available, you may also use instant coconut powder or coconut cream. For the best results, it is important to follow the directions given on the container.

CHILLIES

There are several varieties of chillies:

Big, red chillies contain fewer seeds and a lot of water, and are not too hot. *Green chillies* are unripe red chillies.

Curly red chillies have many seeds, are hot, but contain less water. These can last long if frozen.

Bird's eye chillies are green when young and red when mature. The smaller the chillies, the hotter they taste.

Dried chillies are preserved ones. To preserve them, choose fresh chillies and steam for 10 minutes. Then dry in the sun until completely dried, and store in an airtight jar.

To reduce the heat of chillies, choose 250 grams big fresh chillies and rub each one with both hands to loosen the seeds. Slice them thinly, put in a bowl and add 1 tablespoon salt. Mix well and knead, then let the mixture stand for 30 minutes. Rinse the sliced chillies a few times with plenty of water, making sure the seeds are removed. Finally, drain and dry with a paper towel. The chillies are now ready to be ground.

ONIONS AND GARLIC

Shallots have a strong aroma and taste. Slice them thinly before pounding. Shallots can be replaced with double the amount of onions.

Garlic is not very often used in Indonesian cuisine. When not pounded with other ingredients, it is sliced thinly, or fried till crisp and added to the dish.

SUGAR

Indonesian cuisine uses sugar obtained from coconut, *enau* or *lontar* (palm-like trees). This type of sugar has a firm shape, and is made from the juice of coconut, *enau* or *lontar* flowers. The juice is extracted by making incisions in the flower. It is cooked until it thickens and poured into moulds.

Palm sugar is also made from this juice but comes in the form of brown granules.

SOUR FLAVOUR

Several ingredients can be used to add a sour taste and tangy aroma to Indonesian dishes.

Tamarind: this grows on Java and Madura. Its pulp is light brown. When kept, the pulp gradually darkens. To use it, first soak the required amount in water and squeeze the pulp to extract the juice. Strain the liquid before adding it to the dish. When using young or unripe tamarind, wash it and boil until tender. Let it cool and peel off the skin to obtain the pulp. Squeeze to extract the juice, then strain.

Asam gelugur (*Garcinia atnoviridis*): The fruit, which is round, like a tangerine, is usually sliced thinly and dried in the sun. Light brown when fresh, it gradually turns darker as it ages. It has an aromatic flavour and does not discolour the sauce or gravy. In some places it is called dried tamarind skin.

Dried sour fruit (*Garcinia cambogia*): the fruit, which looks like dark green lime, is sliced into half, and the seeds and flesh are removed before the peel is dried until it turns dark. This has a slightly bitter taste. Usually 1–2 pieces are used as flavouring.

Salted dried carambola: used in Aceh cuisine, salted dried carambola has a mildly sour taste and is usually pounded with other ingredients.

Lime: choose ripe yellow limes to obtain more juice. Quarter the fruit and discard the seeds. The peel can also give an aromatic flavour to your dish. Peel off the thin white skin because this makes your dish taste bitter.

Dark green lime (*kesturi*) is smaller than lime and has a distinctive aroma.

Cui lemon: in Sumatra this is known as *kacau* lime; in the Philippines, it is called calamansi. It looks like lime but has a smoother surface. It tastes sour and has a fragrant aroma.

Carambola: this tastes fresh and sour. It is usually thinly sliced or halved lengthwise. If you are using a lot of carambolas, add salt, squeeze, then rinse to reduce the sour taste.

Dried shrimp paste

Black shrimp paste

Ready-to-use
dried shrimp paste

Soy sauce

Rebon

Dried shrimps

SEASONINGS

Dried shrimp paste: this is made from fresh small shrimps, which are fermented for 2–3 days, then ground with salt and dried. It is sold raw, so it has to be cooked by toasting, roasting, frying or steaming. Cook this in a large amount, then store in an airtight jar and freeze.

Dried shrimps: these are boiled prawns that have been peeled and dried.

Rinse before use then roast or fry until dried. You can use them whole or pounded. They can be added to the sauce mixture for *empek-empek* (fried fish dough) or *asinan* (salted vegetables or fruit mixture).

Rebon: these are small, dried, salted shrimps.

Black shrimp or fish paste: made from seasoned shrimp or fresh fish stock

which is cooked until the stock becomes thick and dark. Shrimp paste is black and sweet while fish paste is brown and salty. Store the paste in a freezer to prevent it from becoming mouldy.

Soy sauce: introduced by the Chinese, this is made from fermented cooked soybeans. Sweet soy sauce contains sugar and has a dark colour and a thick consistency.

Bean curd

Fermented soybean

Egg noodles

Glass noodles

Vermicelli

Fermented
soybean waste

FERMENTED SOYBEAN (Tempe)

A common food on Java island, this is made from cooked soybeans fermented with yeast. Good-quality fermented soybean is covered with white fungi and has a distinctive aroma. If the fermented soybean is stored at a high temperature, this aroma will change. The cake is then called *tempe semangit* or *tempe bosok* (over-fermented soybean) and is used as a seasoning for *sayur lodeh* (mixed vegetables in coconut milk).

FERMENTED SOYBEAN WASTE

(Oncom)

A product from West Java, this is made from nut or soybean waste from which oil has been extracted. It is then fermented like *tempe*.

Two characteristics of *oncom* are its distinctive aroma and reddish fungus wrapping. *Oncom* from soybean waste has a thick fungus wrapping.

BEAN CURD (Tahu)

Introduced by the Chinese, bean curd is produced from concentrate soybean juice. There are several types:

Cotton bean curd is a white, hard bean curd cake formed after soybean concentrate has been strained through cotton fabric.

Water or silk bean curd has a soft texture that breaks easily. Water bean curd is usually not deep-fried.

Yellow bean curd is made the same way as cotton bean curd, but this variety is thinner and is soaked in turmeric juice.

Deep-fried bean curd: this is a firm bean curd that is fried before it is sold in the market.

NOODLES

Noodles have been produced by the Chinese since 100 B.C., and brought by Marco Polo to Italy and the Middle East countries as pasta.

Egg noodles are usually made from flour and can be found fresh or dried.

Vermicelli: made from rice flour, this is finer and has a brittle texture in its dried form. Before using vermicelli, soak it in cold water until tender, or in hot water for a few minutes. Similar to vermicelli are *glass noodles*, made from mung bean flour. Before using it, cut and soak until tender, then drain.

Herbs, Spices & Seasonings

~

As with other Asian cuisine, Indonesian dishes are rich with spices and seasonings. Almost every Asian spice and seasoning can be found in the gourmet sections of big supermarkets or at Asian food stores. These spices can be used fresh in form of roots or leaves, or dried in the form of seeds or corns. If fresh spices and seasonings are not available, use the powdered form usually sold in bottles as a substitute.

GALANGAL (*Lengkuas*)

This rhizome has many joints. To use, first rinse it thoroughly. Cut a piece 1 cm thick, scrape the skin off and bruise, chop coarsely or grind as required. You may also use dried galangal. To prepare them, first rinse and scrape the skin off. Cut thinly, then dry in the sun until completely dried. Store in an airtight container. Before using, soak the galangal for 10 minutes in hot water.

1 tablespoon chopped galangal = 1 teaspoon powdered galangal

LESSER GALANGAL (*Kencur*)

It gives a distinctive aroma and taste to certain dishes, such as *sambal pecek*, *rempeyek* (savoury peanut wafer), *lodeh* (vegetables in coconut milk), spiced grated coconut for vegetable salad, etc.

You only need a small amount of fresh, dried or powdered lesser galangal.

1 teaspoon chopped lesser galangal = 1/2 teaspoon powdered lesser galangal.

GINGER (*Jahe*)

Ripe ginger is hotter than an unripe one. Used to season dishes and to give it a fragrant aroma, ginger also eliminates the unpleasant smell of fish, meat or chicken.

Ginger can be used fresh, dried or in powdered form.

1 teaspoon chopped ginger = 1/4 teaspoon powdered ginger.

LESSER GINGER (*Temu Kunci*)

Its unique aroma can eliminate the putrid odour of fish. Use it sliced, chopped or ground.

TURMERIC (*Kunyit*)

Giving food a yellow colour, this is usually used fresh, dried or in powdered form.

1 tablespoon chopped turmeric = 1/4 teaspoon powdered turmeric.

TEMU MANGGA

Like turmeric, this adds a yellow colour, albeit lighter, to dishes and has a fresh aroma. It can be used fresh, dried or in powdered form.

1 tablespoon chopped *temu mangga* = 1/2 teaspoon powdered *temu mangga*.

KAFFIR LIME LEAF

(Daun Jeruk Purut)
Used fresh or dried, this gives a fresh aroma to *gulai* dishes (dishes cooked with coconut milk) and to curry. Before using, remove the main vein and tear or thinly slice the leaf.

LEMON GRASS *(Daun Serai)*
Only the white or light green portion of a fresh lemon grass is used. Used bruised, ground or sliced thinly, this gives dishes a fresh and fragrant aroma.

BASIL LEAF *(Daun Kemangi)*
This slightly curly leaf with a strong aroma is known as *ruku-ruku* or *selasih* in Sumatra. It is used in fish dishes. The wider and smaller leaves are used in dishes or eaten fresh as salad.

PANDANUS LEAF *(Daun Pandan)*
This soft fragrant leaf is used in North Sulawesi to wrap *ketupat* (compressed rice cakes). In other provinces, the pandanus leaf is added when cooking rice. You can also grind or pound the leaf and extract the green juice to colour your dishes.

SALAM LEAF *(Daun Salam)*
This can be used fresh or dried. You may use laurel leaf or bay leaf as a substitute, or do not use any at all, since it does not really affect the taste or aroma of your dish.

CUMIN LEAF *(Daun Jintan)*
Called 'thick leaf' because of its thickness, this has fine hair on its surface and the fragrance of cumin and anise. Thinly sliced cumin leaves is used in North Sulawesi.

SUJI LEAF *(Daun Suji)*
Called *Pandan Betawi*, this leaf is not as fragrant as the pandanus leaf. It is used mainly as a food colouring since it has a darker green colour than the pandanus leaf.

CURRY LEAF

(Daun Salam Koja / Temurui)
In North Sumatra, this small green leaf is used, fresh or dried, in *gulai* (dishes cooked with coconut milk) and curry.

CHIVES *(Daun Kucai)*

Introduced by the Chinese, this has finer leaves than the Western chives. Finely cut chives is often used as a garnish for *soto* (spiced soup), or is stir-fried.

SZECHUAN PEPPER *(Andaliman)*

Like fresh pepper, this has a pleasant aroma and tastes hot and spicy. It is used in Batak (North Sumatran) dishes such as *arsik* (dried fish in coconut milk).

TURMERIC LEAF *(Daun Kunyit)*

This long and wide leaf is used in West Sumatran dishes such as *rendang* (beef in coconut milk), *kalio*, etc. Used fresh or dried.

LEEK / SPRING ONION

(Daun Bawang / Prei)
Bakung spring onion (leek) has flat leaves while the spring onion has hollow tube-like leaves. Use only the white or light green portion, since the green portion has an unpleasant smell and contains a little mucus.

PEPPERCORNS *(Merica)*

Indonesian dishes use mainly white peppercorns (ripe peppercorns as compared to black peppercorns which are dried and unripe). Peppercorns are commonly used in Bali and Aceh. It is not too hot, but has an intense aroma. Use whole peppercorns or pepper powder as needed.

CORIANDER *(Ketumbar)*

Coriander is sold whole or in powdered form. It has an intense aroma, especially if pounded. To use, first rinse coriander, then roast before grinding. Store in a cool and airtight container.

1 tablespoon coriander corns = $1/2$ tablespoon coriander powder

CUMIN *(Jintan)*

This is used in *gulai* (dishes cooked with coconut milk) or curry. To use, first rinse, then roast before grinding. Store in a cool and airtight container.

1 teaspoon cumin = $1/2$ teaspoon powdered cumin

CLOVES *(Cengkih)*

Use whole or as a powder.

1 tablespoon cloves = 1 teaspoon powdered cloves

CANDLENUT *(Kemiri)*

This round, cream-coloured nut tastes delicious. Roast or fry before using it to eliminate its unpleasant smell and poison. If unavailable, substitute with macadamia nuts, fried cashews or almonds.

CARDAMOM *(Kapulaga)*

Some are white while others are green with an intense fragrance. Pods may be rounded or elongated. Bruise lightly or grind before using.

NUTMEG & MACE
(Pala & Bunga Pala)

The nutmeg fruit has a hard skin and is covered with a red flower called mace. Both the fruit and mace are dried. Mace is less fragrant than the nutmeg fruit. They are sold and used whole or in powdered form.

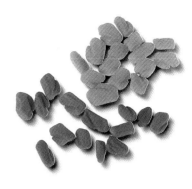

CINNAMON *(Kayu Manis)*
You may use this dried bark whole or as a powder. Where recipes in this book specify the length of bark to be used, e.g. 5 cm, use the dried bark.

STAR ANISE *(Bunga Lawang / Pekak)*
Commonly used in Chinese or Indian dishes, only certain regions in Indonesia use this spice. Shaped like an eight-pointed star, its tips contain flat seeds that have a fragrance similar to the anise seed.

FENUGREEK *(Klabet)*
This grain-shaped, yellowish-orange spice is used in fish curry or *gulai ikan* (fish in coconut milk).

ANISEED *(Adas Manis)*
Similar to cumin, this is as big as a rice grain, and is used in *gulai* (dishes cooked with coconut milk) or curry. Aniseed is not the same as fennel or *pulosari* anise which has almost the same shape. The *pulosari* anise seed has a tail and is used in making medicinal herbs.

POPPY SEEDS *(Kas-kas)*
These are white or blue-black corns. Use white corns to maintain the natural colour of your dish. Its use is the influence of India and the Middle East.

BLACK NUT *(Kluwak)*
Kluwak is used in *rawon* (beef with black sweet sauce), a special dish from East Java. To use it, first break the shell and take out the flesh. Taste it; if it is not bitter, soak it until tender, then grind. *Pucung,* the white flesh of an unripe *kluwak,* is also used as a seasoning. *Pucung* does not alter the colour of your dish, unlike *kluwak,* which darkens it.

Fruits, Buds & Leaves

~

Indonesia is a country rich in edible plants which are delicious as well as nutritious. Unfortunately, most of us do not know how to use or prepare them. This chapter will enlighten you on the techniques of preparation and the use of these delicacies.

AUBERGINE (Terung)

Aubergines, also known as eggplants, come in several varieties:

The long violet aubergine has many seeds while the big round violet variety is sweeter. The skin colour changes when cooked, although the taste does not.

Small violet aubergines are used in Japanese dishes.

The big, green variety is slightly bitter. To reduce the bitterness, rub it with salt and let it stand for 15–20 minutes. Then rinse and drain.

The small and round green aubergine, which can be cooked, is mostly eaten as a salad.

Pea aubergines are small and grow in clusters. These are mostly eaten raw or cooked as part of a vegetable dish.

BITTER GOURD (Pare / Paria)

The bright green bitter gourd has fewer seeds than the pale green variety. Both taste bitter. The bitterness can be reduced by rubbing salt to sliced pieces and squeezing until tender.

SQUASH (Oyong)

This squash-like vegetable has a thick skin, and its flesh and seeds are very soft. Remove the skin or any hard parts before using it.

YOUNG JACKFRUIT (Nangka Muda)

Choose an unripe jackfruit with small seeds and firm flesh. This is usually used in vegetable dishes such as *Sayur Gori* (Jackfruit in Coconut Milk; page 60).

BANANA (Pisang)

Kepok bananas are commonly used in dishes such as *Gangan Asam* (page 68).

Small, green aubergines

Bitter gourd

Young jackfruit

Young bananas

Aubergines

Small, violet aubergines

Pea aubergines

Kepok bananas

Aubergines

CHAYOTE *(Labu Siam)*
Before peeling, cut it in half and let it stand for 30 minutes to let the sticky sap out. Or peel it under running water. Unripe chayotes are boiled and used in a salad.

GANDARIA
Unripe *gandaria* is green while the ripe ones are yellow and tastes like mango. Unripe *gandaria* is used to give a sour and fresh flavour to *sambal*.

VEGETABLE MARROW *(Labu Air)*
This long, round vegetable has a light green skin and contains a lot of water.

WAX GOURD *(Beligo / Kundur)*
A member of the squash family, this fruit is ovalish-round and big, weighing up to 3–4 kilograms. Its dark green skin is flaked with white 'powder'. Besides its use for cooking, the fruit is sliced, dried and sold as *tangkweh* (sugared melon).

PUMPKIN *(Labu Kuning)*
The weight of a pumpkin can go up to 4–5 kilograms. Unripe pumpkin is green, and gradually becomes brown as it matures. Its flesh is yellow.

Another variety is round and flat with dark green skin. It is smaller than an ordinary pumpkin and has firmer flesh. It comes from Japan, where it is known as *Kabucha*.

LEUNCA
Similar to the pea aubergine, this is small, round and dark green. It tastes a little bitter. Used in Sundanese dishes, it is usually eaten raw or mixed with other ingredients.

BAMBOO SHOOTS *(Rebung)*
These are sold as peeled bamboo shoots which taste bitter. They need to be cooked several times, or soaked in the water from washing rice or in plain water for 2–3 nights.

YAM BEAN *(Bengkuang)*
This is used as a substitute for bamboo shoot in many Indonesian dishes such as *Tekwan* soup (Fish Ball Soup).

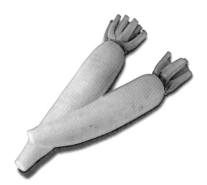

RADISH *(Lobak)*
This Chinese root is also known as *Lo Bok* (*Daikon* in Japanese), and is used in *Soto Bandung* (Bandung soup).

BEAN SPROUTS *(Tauge)*
These come from green beans or soy beans. A day-old sprout, with a shorter and harder stem, is used in a salad. A two-day-old sprout is longer and has a brownish tail which must be removed.

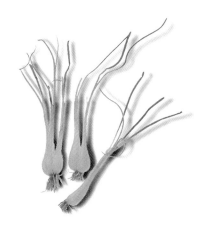

CHINESE CHIVES *(Lokio)*
A member of the shallot family, this has long fine leaves and a delicate taste. Its fragrance is as strong as that of shallots.

PINK GINGER BUD

(Kecombrang Bud)
Pink or red in colour, it is called *honje* in West Java and *kantan* bud in Malaysia. It has a delicate aroma, and is cooked with fish to reduce the smell, or sliced as part of a vegetable salad. In Aceh or Batak, it is known as *palang* bud.

PAPAYA BUD *(Bunga Papaya Gantung)*
The papaya bud, like its leaves, tastes bitter. To reduce the bitterness, boil this with cassava leaves, drain, then mix with spiced grated coconut or cook as desired.

BANANA BUD

(Bunga / Jantung Pisang)
It is called 'banana heart' because its shape is similar to a cow's heart. Only *kepok* or *batu* banana buds are delicious. They are usually made into a salad, mixed with spiced peanut sauce, or cooked in coconut milk.

BLACK CHINESE MUSHROOM

(Jamur Kuping)
This is used in *Tekwan Soup* (Fish Ball Soup) or *Kimlo* (Mixed Vegetable Soup). Usually sold dried. Soak until tender before using.

LILY BUD *(Bunga Sedap Malam)*

Similar to the dried banana bud, its use is the influence of China. Soak until tender before using it, then tie a knot and mix in *Kimlo* soup.

CHINESE PARSLEY *(Seledri)*

There are two kinds of celery—with small stems and leaves and with big and wide stems and leaves. Both varieties have the same taste and aroma.

KENIKIR LEAVES *(Daun Kenikir)*

Fragrant, with a bitter taste, the ones with pinkish buds which are less bitter are usually selected for salad or cooking.

KATUK LEAVES

(Daun Katuk / Nasi-nasi)

These are small and hard dark green leaves, said to be good for breast-feeding mothers.

CUP LEAVES

(Daun Mangkukan / Tapak Liman)

Young cup leaves are boiled for vegetable salad, or torn / sliced to be added to fish *gulai* (fish in coconut milk) or brain *gulai* to reduce the smell. Cup leaves have a delicate aroma, and as an ingredient in hair oil.

FERNTOPS *(Daun Pakis)*

Choose edible, young ferns which have curly tips and are soft. In America, edible ferns can be eaten raw. They are related to the fiddlehead fern. After washing the fern leaves, they should be dried until soft to get rid of the mucus.

RICE & NOODLES

Nasi Kunyit

(Turmeric Glutinous Rice)
~

500	grams glutinous rice, soaked for at least 2 hours, drained
1	tablespoon shredded turmeric or $^1/_2$ teaspoon powdered turmeric
125	cc thick coconut milk
$^1/_2$	tablespoon salt
2	pandanus leaves, torn and knotted
1	teaspoon lime juice (to enhance the yellow colour of turmeric)

Steam glutinous rice for 15 minutes until it is half-cooked, then remove to another saucepan. ❧ Dissolve shredded turmeric in coconut milk and strain the liquid. Bring to the boil coconut milk with salt and pandanus leaves. ❧ Pour the boiled coconut milk onto the glutinous rice and allow to simmer. Stir occasionally until the milk is completely absorbed. ❧ Add lime juice, mix well and steam until cooked.

Note: In Sumatra, Nasi Kunyit is served with Yellow Spiced Grilled Chicken (page 82) or unti (shredded coconut mixed with brown sugar) as the main dish in a traditional ceremony such as a wedding ceremony. After the ceremony, the turmeric rice will be shared among the guests.

Nasi Kuning

(Yellow Rice)
~

800	grams rice
2	tablespoons shredded turmeric or 1 tablespoon powdered turmeric
1	litre coconut milk from 1 coconut (discard the skin)
1	tablespoon salt
2	*salam* leaves (or bay leaves as a substitute)
2	stalks lemon grass, bruised
1	tablespoon lime juice

Serve with:
- **Opor Ayam (Chicken in Coconut Milk)** ... page 90
- **Sambal Goreng Kreni (Meat Balls in Coconut Milk)** ... page 110
- **Kering Tempe (Fried Fermented Soybean)** ... page 170
- **fried black soybeans**
- **thin omelette**
- **spicy coconut balls**
- ***abon daging (dried shredded beef)***
- **cucumber**

Wash and drain rice. Steam for 25 minutes until it is half-cooked, then remove to another saucepan. ❧ Soak the shredded turmeric in coconut milk and bring to the boil with salt, *salam* leaves and lemon grass. ❧ Pour the boiled coconut milk onto the half-cooked rice, add lime juice and allow to simmer. Continue to stir until the liquid is completely absorbed. Then steam until thoroughly cooked.

Fried Black Soybeans: Blanch 100 grams black soy beans with boiling water, then drain. After it has cooled, combine the soybeans with 1 teaspoon salt and fry with oil until it is thoroughly cooked. Drain.

Thin Omelette: Beat 2 eggs with $1^1/_2$ tablespoons water and $^1/_4$ teaspoon salt. Fry the eggs to make a thin omelette, roll it up and slice thinly.

Spicy Coconut Balls: Grind $^1/_2$ red chilli pepper, $^1/_2$ teaspoon chopped lesser galangal, 1 kaffir lime leaf, $^1/_2$ teaspoon roasted coriander, 1 clove garlic, 1 shallot and $^1/_2$ teaspoon salt. Combine the ground spices with $^1/_4$ shredded coconut (skin removed), 1 tablespoon finely minced beef and $^1/_2$ egg. Make into balls, flatten slightly and fry until golden brown.

Note: For almost every traditional ceremony or special occasion, the Javanese serve Yellow Rice complete with its accompanying dishes.

Opposite: (From left) Nasi Kuning and Nasi Kunyit

Nasi Langgi
(Steamed Rice in Spiced Coconut Milk)

500	grams rice
450	cc coconut milk from $1/2$ coconut
3	cm galangal
1	teaspoon coriander, roasted
$1/2$	teaspoon salt

Spices (ground):
2	cloves garlic
5	shallots
1	teaspoon coriander, roasted

Serve with:
  terik daging (beef in coconut milk)
  fried fermented soybean
  serundeng kelapa (spiced grated coconut)
  cabai udang goreng (spicy fried shrimps)
  thinly sliced omelette
  basil and thinly sliced cucumber

Wash rice and steam for 25 minutes until half-cooked. ✦ Bring to the boil coconut milk with ground spices, galangal, lemon grass and salt. Add the half-cooked rice to the coconut milk and cook until the milk is completely absorbed. Steam until cooked. ✦ Put other dishes on top of the rice or surrounding it. Serve on a plate or banana leaf.

Terik Daging: Grind 1 teaspoon coriander, $1/2$ teaspoon cumin, 5 shallots and 1 clove garlic. With 3 tablespoons oil, sauté ground spices until fragrant and dry. Add lightly bruised lemon grass, 1 cm bruised galangal, 2 salam leaves and 500 grams beef. Mix well. Add 750 cc coconut milk from half a coconut, 1 teaspoon salt, 1 teaspoon tamarind juice and a little brown sugar. Simmer over low heat until the coconut milk is completely absorbed and the beef is tender.

Fried Fermented Soybean: Slice finely 2 red chillies, 5 shallots and 2 cloves garlic, 2 salam leaves, and 1 cm bruised galangal. With 3 tablespoons oil, sauté with $1/2$ teaspoon dried shrimp paste until fragrant and soft. ✦ Add 250 grams chopped fermented soybean (tempe) and mix well. Add 250 cc water, 1 teaspoon salt, 1 tablespoon sweet soy sauce, 1 teaspoon tamarind juice and a little brown sugar. Simmer over low heat until the water is completely absorbed.

Serundeng Kelapa: Grate half a coconut (skin removed). Grind 1 teaspoon coriander, 5 shallots, 2 cloves garlic, brown sugar, $1/2$ teaspoon salt and 1 teaspoon tamarind juice. Mix well with the grated coconut. Add 1 cm bruised galangal, 2 salam leaves and 1 stalk lemon grass. Sauté all ingredients over medium heat. Fry until the ingredients are fairly dry.

Cabai Udang Goreng: Finely slice 10 seeded red chillies, 5 shallots, 2 cloves garlic, 1 cm bruised galangal and 2 salam leaves. With 3 tablespoons oil, sauté the spices until fragrant and soft. Add 250 grams shelled shrimps and mix well. Add $1/2$ teaspoon salt and sauté until the colour changes.

Nasi Uduk
(Steamed Rice in Coconut Milk)

500	grams rice
600	cc coconut milk
$1/2$	tablespoon salt
2	salam leaves (or bay leaves as a substitute)
2	pandanus leaves, torn and knotted
1	teaspoon powdered coriander

Peanut Sauce:
100	grams peanuts, fried
1	red chilli
10	bird's eye chillies
1	teaspoon salt
1	tablespoon sugar
1	tablespoon vinegar
150	cc water

Serve with:
  fried small salted fish (teri nasi)
  fried peanuts
  finely sliced omelette
  fried shallots
  fried melinjo nut crackers
  peanut sauce

Wash rice and steam for 25 minutes until half-cooked. ✦ Bring to the boil coconut milk with salt, salam and pandanus leaves and coriander. Remove rice from the steamer and put in a pan. Add boiled coconut milk until it covers the rice and simmer over low heat until the milk is completely absorbed. Steam again until cooked. ✦ Grind and mix all ingredients for peanut sauce. ✦ Serve rice with other dishes and peanut sauce.

Opposite: (From left) Nasi Langgi and Nasi Uduk
Following pages: (Clockwise from top) Cabai Goreng Udang,
Serundeng Kelapa and Terik Daging

Nasi Pundhut

(Coconut Milk Rice in Banana Leaf)
~

750	grams rice
1	litre thin coconut milk
2	*salam* leaves (or bay leaves as a substitute)
1/2	tablespoon salt
200	cc thick coconut milk
	banana leaves

Serve with:
Telur Pindang (Eggs Boiled with Spices and Herbs) ...
   page 186
sambal bajak

Wash and steam rice for 20 minutes until half-cooked. Bring to the boil thin coconut milk with *salam* leaves and salt. Put the half-cooked rice into another saucepan and add boiling coconut milk. Simmer over low heat, stirring occasionally until the coconut milk is absorbed. ❧ Season the thick coconut milk with a little salt. Put 4–5 tablespoons rice on 2 banana leaves and pour 2–3 tablespoons thick coconut milk over it. Wrap the banana leaves around the rice and secure both ends with toothpicks. ❧ Steam for about 45 minutes until cooked. Serve with *Telur Pindang* and *sambal bajak*.

Sambal Bajak: Grind 10 seeded chillies, 5 shallots, 1 teaspoon dried shrimp paste, 2 cloves garlic, 1/2 teaspoon salt, 1 tablespoon brown sugar and 3 candlenuts. Sauté with 5 tablespoons oil until fragrant and dry.

Tinotuan / Bubur Manado

(Manado Vegetable Porridge)
~

250	grams rice, washed and drained
200	grams pumpkin, chopped
100	grams sweet potato, chopped
1	cob sweetcorn, extract the kernels
50	grams young melinjo leaves
50	grams spinach, washed
50	grams water convolvulus, washed
5–6	string beans, cut into 2 cm pieces
2	teaspoons salt

Serve with:
sambal dabu-dabu lilang
grilled fish
fried salted fish

Add water to a level 3–5 cm above the rice level. Boil until almost cooked. Add pumpkin, sweet potato and corn. When they are cooked, add vegetables and salt. Cook until the cereal thickens. Serve with *sambal dabu-dabu lilang* and grilled fish or fried salted fish.

Sambal Dabu-dabu Lilang: Finely slice 4 red chillies, 6 bird's eye chillies and 3 shallots. Mix well with 1 chopped tomato, 1 tablespoon lime juice and 1/2 teaspoon salt.

Grilled Fish: Wash tuna fish (500 grams) and rub with 1/2 teaspoon salt, 1/2 teaspoon shredded ginger and 2 tablespoons vegetable oil. Grill until cooked.

Fried Salted Fish: Cut 150 grams salted fish into 2 x 2 cm pieces and soak with boiling water. Let it stand until cooled. Wash, pat it dry, then fry.

Opposite: (Clockwise from top) Tinotuan, Nasi Pundhut, Sambal Bajak, Telur Pindang, Fried Salted Fish and Sambal Dabu-dabu Lilang

Arem-arem
(Steamed Rice with Beef)
~

3	tablespoons oil
350	grams minced beef
300	cc thick coconut milk from $2/3$ coconut
500	grams rice, washed and drained
1	litre thin coconut milk from $1/2$ coconut
1	teaspoon salt
2	*salam* leaves (or bay leaves as a substitute)
	banana leaves, for wrapping

Spices (ground):

5	red chillies
1	teaspoon chopped lesser galangal
3	cloves garlic
6	shallots
2	tomatoes, chopped
2	teaspoons chopped galangal
2	teaspoons sugar
1	teaspoon salt

Sauté ground spices in oil until fragrant, then add minced beef. Stir until excess juice from the beef is absorbed, then pour in thick coconut milk. Boil until the beef is tender and the gravy is completely absorbed. Remove and allow to cool. ❧ Put rice in a saucepan and add thin coconut milk, salt and *salam* leaves. Cook until the coconut milk is absorbed completely and the rice becomes tender. Allow to cool. ❧ Fill one banana leaf with 2 tablespoons rice. Flatten to 1 cm thickness. Add 1–2 tablespoons beef, roll up the banana leaf and secure both ends with toothpicks. (Each *arem-arem* should be about 10 cm long, with a diameter $2^1/_2$ cm). ❧ Steam for about 1 hour until cooked. Allow to cool before serving.

Buras
(Steamed Rice with Herbs)
~

500	grams rice, washed and drained
1	litre coconut milk
2	teaspoons salt
2	*salam* leaves (or bay leaves as a substitute)
	banana leaves, for wrapping
	string, for tying

Boil rice, coconut milk, salt and *salam* leaves until the rice is half-cooked and tender. ❧ Fill one banana leaf with 2–3 tablespoons rice, roll up and fold both ends. (Each *buras* should be approximately 8 x 5 cm). ❧ Take 2 *buras*, arrange them with folds facing each other on the inside and tie with a string in 3 places. Steam for about 1 hour until cooked. ❧ Untie the strings and serve with *sambal poyak*.

Sambal Poyak: Roast 150 grams shredded coconut with 1 teaspoon chopped lesser galangal, 2 kaffir lime leaves and 2 thinly sliced red chillies. Add $1/2$ teaspoon salt and 1 teaspoon sugar, and pound coarsely.

Opposite: (From left) Buras and Arem-arem

Nasi Goreng
(Fried Rice)
~

5	tablespoons oil
600	grams refrigerated rice
1–2	tablespoons sweet soy sauce

Spices (ground):

5	shallots
3	cloves garlic
3–5	red chillies
1/2	teaspoon dried shrimp paste

Sauté ground spices in oil until fragrant and thoroughly cooked. Add rice and sweet soy sauce. Mix well until rice becomes warm. ❖ Serve fried rice with fried eggs, finely sliced cucumber and fried shallots.

Betawi Fried Rice: Add 150 grams chopped lamb to the cooked spices and fry until cooked.

Note: Use cooled rice, preferably rice that has been left overnight, to make fried rice. Newly-cooked rice breaks easily and sticks to the frying pan.

Ketupat Ketan
(Steamed Glutinous Compressed Rice Cakes)
~

20	small *ketupat* wraps (made from coconut leaves)
800	grams white glutinous rice, washed and drained
2 1/2	litres coconut milk from 2 coconuts
2	tablespoons salt

Fill *ketupat* wraps with glutinous rice until nearly full (about 1 cm from one edge of the wrap). ❖ Put them in a saucepan, cover with coconut milk and add salt. ❖ Boil for 2–3 hours until *ketupat* is cooked and coconut milk is completely absorbed. Excess oil seeps out, so the *ketupat* will look as though it has been fried. ❖ Unwrap, cut and serve with durian, fried banana, a savoury dish such as *Rendang Daging* (Beef in Spicy Coconut Milk, page 118), or *tape ketan* (a sweet black glutinous rice bought at Malay or Indonesian cake stalls).

Opposite: (Clockwise from top) Tepo (page 38), Ketupat Ketan, tape ketan and a serving of ketupat with curry

Above: Nasi Goreng

Ketupat and Lontong Beras
(Compressed Rice Cakes and Rice Dumplings)
~

Ketupat (Compressed Rice Cakes):
500	grams rice, washed and drained
Approx. 8	medium-sized *ketupat* wraps

Fill *ketupat* wraps with rice until one-third full. Put them in a saucepan and cover with water. ❧ Boil for 3–4 hours until thoroughly cooked. Add boiling water if the water level gets too low. ❧ To clean cooked *ketupat*, wash with cold water, then drain and allow to cool.

Lontong (Rice Dumplings):
500	grams rice, washed and drained
Approx. 8	banana leaves, 25 x 30 cm (bigger leaves preferred)

Before wrapping rice, plunge the banana leaves in boiling water for about 2 seconds so that it softens and will not break easily. Pat it dry before using. ❧ Roll up each leaf with the dark green side facing up. Each should have a diameter of 3 cm. Secure one end with toothpicks. ❧ Fill every rolled-up leaf with rice until half-full. Secure the other end, put in a saucepan, and cover with water. Bring to the boil. ❧ The method of cooking *lontong* is similar to cooking *ketupat*. When the *lontong* is cooked, put it upright until it has completely drained, cooled and hardened.

Note: Ketupat and lontong serve the same function as rice in Indonesian dishes. ❧ In Sulawesi, the ketupat wrap is made from pandanus leaves or from young coconut leaves. ❧ Substitute the ketupat / lontong wrap with a muslin bag if you prefer the colour of the ketupat or lontong to remain white. You may also use a lontong container, which is a tin tube with small holes in its surface. ❧ To reduce cooking time, use half-cooked rice. Fill the container to two-thirds full, then boil for 2 hours.

Tepo (Java): Take 2 banana leaves, the green sides facing up and fold such that it becomes a container (*pincuk*). Fill the *pincuk* with rice until it is one-third or two-thirds full. Fold the left and right sides, secure with toothpicks and boil as described above.

Opposite: (From left) Lontong and Ketupat served with Rawon (Brisket in Black Nut Sauce, page 114)

Roti Jala

(Lacy Pancakes)
~

250	grams flour
1/2	teaspoon salt
2	eggs, lightly beaten
500	cc coconut milk / water
1	tablespoon oil / melted butter

Mix flour, salt and beaten eggs. Still stirring, add coconut milk gradually to get a smooth mixture. Strain if necessary. Pour in some oil, and stir until mixed completely. ❧ Make the pancakes by using a special cup with 4 narrow spouts in the bottom to get the lacy effect. Heat a flat frying pan and grease lightly with oil. Scoop up the batter with the cup. Swirl it in the frying pan in circles so that it forms a lacy pancake. Allow pancake to set on top, then turn over and cook. Continue cooking until all the batter has been used up. ❧ Fold in the sides of the pancake and roll up. Serve hot.

Roti Cane

(Light Flaky Bread)
~

175	grams flour
1/2	teaspoon salt
100	cc warm water
125	grams melted butter / margarine

Knead flour, salt and warm water into a dough. Add melted butter or margarine and knead until smooth. Divide into 8–10 parts, then roll each piece into a ball. Allow to stand for about 15 minutes. ❧ Flatten to about 1/2 cm thickness, then put into a flat, lightly-oiled frying pan. Fry each pancake, turning over frequently, until it is cooked.

Mi Goreng Jawa

(Javanese Fried Noodles)
~

250	grams egg noodles or 150 grams dried noodles
3–5	tablespoons oil
150	grams beef, boiled, cut into 1 cm cubes or fried chicken, shredded
100	grams shrimps, shelled
150	cc stock
2–3	tablespoons sweet soy sauce
2	cabbage leaves, cut into 1/2 cm pieces
2	spring onions, finely sliced
100	grams bean sprouts, tailed
1	sprig Chinese parsley, finely sliced
1–2	tablespoons fried shallots
	fried melinjo nut crackers

Spices (ground):

3	candlenuts, fried / roasted
3	cloves garlic
1	teaspoon peppercorns
1/2	teaspoon salt

Blanch noodles with hot water until tender. Drain and set aside. ❧ Sauté ground spices in oil until golden brown, then add beef and shrimps. Stir until shrimps change colour, then pour in the stock. Bring to the boil, and add sweet soy sauce, cabbage, noodles and spring onions. ❧ Add bean sprouts and Chinese parsley, and mix well. Continue cooking until the stock is completely absorbed. Sprinkle with fried shallots and melinjo nut crackers.

Opposite: (On a plate, from top) Roti Cane and Roti Jala, served with a bowl of Kari Kambing (page 128)

Bihun Goreng
(Fried Vermicelli)
~

250	grams dried vermicelli
5	tablespoons oil
5	cloves garlic, finely chopped
250	grams chicken, finely sliced
200	grams shrimps, shelled and deveined
100	grams carrots, thinly sliced
125	cc stock / water
3	cabbage leaves, cut into 1/2 cm pieces
150	grams Chinese cabbage, cut into 3 cm pieces
50	grams snow peas, cut the ends
2	spring onions, cut into 3 cm pieces
2	sprigs Chinese parsley, cut into 2 cm pieces
2	tablespoons salty soy sauce
4	tablespoons sweet soy sauce
1/2	teaspoon pepper
1	teaspoon salt

Blanch the dried vermicelli with hot water until tender. Drain, then set aside. ↝ Sauté garlic in oil until golden brown, then add chicken, shrimps and carrots. Stir until the shrimps change colour. Pour in the stock and bring to the boil. ↝ Add vegetables, soy sauces, pepper, salt and vermicelli. Mix well until the stock is completely absorbed. ↝ Serve hot with a sprinkle of fried shallots.

Laksa
(Rich Noodle Soup)
~

200	grams dried vermicelli
3	tablespoons oil
2	*salam* leaves (or bay leaves as a substitute)
1	stalk lemon grass, bruised
250	grams shrimps, shelled
1 1/2	litres coconut milk from 1 coconut
2	tablespoons shredded coconut, roasted until golden brown, pounded
200	grams bean sprouts, tailed, blanched, drained
1	chicken (850 grams), boiled, shredded
4	eggs, boiled, shelled, cut into 8 pieces
2–3	tablespoons fried shallots
50	grams basil leaves

Spices (ground):

1	tablespoon coriander, roasted
3	cloves garlic
7	shallots
2	teaspoons chopped galangal
2	teaspoons chopped *temu mangga / temu pao* or 1 teaspoon chopped turmeric
3	candlenuts, roasted
2	teaspoons salt
1	teaspoon sugar

Blanch the dried vermicelli with hot water until tender. Drain, then set aside. ↝ Heat the oil and sauté ground spices, *salam* leaves and lemon grass until fragrant. Add shrimps, coconut milk and pounded coconut. Bring to the boil and stir occasionally to prevent the coconut milk from curdling.

Sambal: Grind 10 red chillies and 2 boiled bird's eye chillies with 1 teaspoon lime juice.

How to serve: Arrange vermicelli, bean sprouts, chicken and sliced eggs in a bowl. Pour hot gravy to cover these and sprinkle with fried shallots and basil. Serve with *sambal*.

Note: *Temu mangga or temu pao gives a soft yellow colour and has a delicious mango aroma. Use 1 teaspoon chopped turmeric as a substitute.*

Opposite: (Clockwise from top) Laksa, Bihun Goreng and Mi Goreng Jawa (page 40)

Mi Lontong
(Rice Dumplings with Noodles)

6–7	*lontong* (rice dumplings)
250	grams egg noodles, covered with boiled water, drained
8	pieces fried bean curd, chopped
150	grams bean sprouts, blanched, drained
1	tablespoon finely sliced Chinese parsley
8	pieces rice crackers
	fried shallots

Sweet Soy Sauce:

5	cloves garlic, sliced, fried
5	bird's eye chillies, thinly sliced
100	cc hot water
4	tablespoons sweet soy sauce
	salt, sugar and vinegar

Sauce: Mix all the ingredients for the sauce.

How to serve: Cut rice dumplings and arrange in a bowl. Add noodles, bean curd, bean sprouts and sliced Chinese parsley. Cover with sauce. Add rice crackers and fried shallots.

Rujak Juhi
(Noodles and Dried Squid Salad)

	lettuce, sliced
250	grams egg noodles, washed and steamed for about 10 minutes
2	pieces bean curd (8 x 8 cm), fried until golden brown, drained and sliced
2	boiled potatoes (200 grams), peeled, sliced and fried until golden brown
1-2	cucumbers, cut into thick slices
100	grams *juhi* (dried squid), washed and fried or roasted
	tapioca crackers, fried
	sweet soy sauce

Peanut Sauce:

200	grams peanuts, fried
5	red chillies
10	bird's eye chillies
1	clove garlic
1–2	tablespoons sugar
1	teaspoon salt
250	cc water
1–2	tablespoons vinegar
	sweet soy sauce

Peanut Sauce: Grind the first five ingredients and mix with water, vinegar and sweet soy sauce. Bring to the boil.

How to serve: Put sliced lettuce on a plate and arrange noodles, bean curd, potato and cucumber slices and dried squid on top. Pour peanut sauce over, adding more sweet soy sauce if desired and garnish with tapioca crackers.

Opposite: (From left) Rujak Juhi and Mi Lontong

Ketoprak
(Bean Curd and Vermicelli with Peanut Sauce)

8	pieces bean curd (5 x 5 cm)
	sweet soy sauce
2	whole *lontong*, 20 x 3 cm, sliced round
100	grams dried vermicelli, blanched, drained
150	grams bean sprouts, tailed, blanched, drained
	fried shallots
	Chinese parsley, chopped
100	grams tapioca crackers / melinjo nut crackers

Spices (ground):

3	cloves garlic
5	bird's eye chillies
1	red chilli
50	grams peanuts, roasted / fried
1–2	teaspoons vinegar
50	cc water

Fry bean curd until golden brown, then drain and chop finely. ❧ Mix ground spices and add sweet soy sauce.

How to serve: Arrange *lontong* (rice dumplings), vermicelli, bean curd, bean sprouts, fried shallots and Chinese parsley on a serving dish. Pour the peanut sauce over and sprinkle with more fried shallots and tapioca crackers or melinjo nut crackers.

Mi Kocok
(Noodles in Shrimp Gravy)

200	grams small shrimps, shelled, set aside the shells
300	cc water
2	tablespoons oil
3	cloves garlic, ground
5	shallots, ground
250	cc chicken stock
1/2	nutmeg, bruised
2	cloves
2	teaspoons finely chopped ginger, ground
1/2	teaspoon pepper
	salt and sugar
75	grams rice flour, mixed with a little water
1/4	chicken, boiled until tender, cut into 1/2 cm cubes
250	grams dried noodles, blanched until tender, drained
100	grams bean sprouts, blanched, drained
1	piece Chinese bean curd (*tofu*), fried until golden brown, cut into 1 cm cubes
2	sprigs Chinese parsley, chopped
3	eggs, boiled, peeled, quartered
	fried shallots
	tapioca crackers
	lime, sliced

Shrimp Stock: Wash shrimp shells and fry in a dry pan until the colour changes. Pour in 300 cc water and simmer over low heat for 30 minutes until the water has reduced to 250 cc. Strain the stock. ❧ Heat the oil and sauté garlic and shallots until golden brown. Pour in both chicken stock and shrimp stock. Add nutmeg, cloves, ginger, pepper, salt, sugar and shrimps. Add rice flour paste to thicken the gravy.

Sambal: Grind 5 red chillies and 10 bird's eye chillies with 50 cc water.

How to serve: Arrange chicken, noodles, bean sprouts, *tofu*, Chinese parsley and eggs in a bowl. Pour the hot gravy over and sprinkle with fried shallots and crackers. Serve hot with *sambal* and lime slices.

Opposite: (From left) Ketoprak and Mi Kocok

VEGETABLES

50 *Gado-gado*
Mixed Vegetable Salad with Peanut Sauce—JAKARTA

Rujak Pengantin
Vegetable Salad with Tangy Peanut Sauce—JAKARTA

Urap Sayuran
Mixed Vegetable Salad with Spiced Grated Coconut—CENTRAL JAVA

52 *Keredok*
Fresh Vegetable Salad with Peanut Sauce—WEST JAVA

Rujak Cingur
Mixed Vegetable Salad with Black Shrimp Paste Sauce—EAST JAVA

54 *Pecel*
Mixed Vegetable Salad with Spicy Peanut Sauce—CENTRAL JAVA

Anyang Pakis
Ferntop Salad with Roasted Coconut —SUMATRA

Selada Banjar
Vegetable Salad with Potato Sauce —KALIMANTAN

56 *Gulai Buncis*
French Beans Curry—SUMATRA

Gulai Daun Paranci
Cassava Leaves and Salted Fish Curry —SUMATRA

Gulai Pakis
Ferntops and Green Beans Curry —SUMATRA

58 *Gulai Silalab*
Cassava Leaves and Pea Aubergines Curry—NORTH SUMATRA

Gulai Manis
Sweet Cabbage Curry—SUMATRA

60 *Sayur Rebung Asam*
Sour Bamboo Shoots Soup—SUMATRA

Sayur Lelawar
Young Bamboo Shoots in Coconut Milk—JAVA

Sayur Gori
Jackfruit in Coconut Milk —CENTRAL JAVA

62 *Sayur Campur*
Mixed Vegetables in Clear Soup —TERNATE, HALMAHERA

Sayur Lodeh
Mixed Vegetables in Coconut Milk —CENTRAL JAVA

64 *Sayur Brongkos*
French Beans in Black Nut Gravy —CENTRAL JAVA

Sayur Kare
Vegetable Curry—CENTRAL JAVA

66 *Sayur Podomoro*
Vegetables and Meat in Spiced Coconut Milk—CENTRAL JAVA

Sayur Bubur
Spinach in Coconut Milk —CENTRAL JAVA

Ihutilinanga
Chilli-fried Aubergines in Coconut Milk—GORONTALO, NORTH SULAWESI

68 *Jangan Asem*
Vegetables in Sweet-Sour Gravy —CENTRAL & EAST JAVA

Gangan Asam
Sweet-Sour Vegetable Soup with Fish —KALIMANTAN

Asem-asem Buncis
French Beans in Sweet-Sour Gravy —CENTRAL & EAST JAVA

70 *Tumis Kacang Panjang*
Stir-fried String Beans in Coconut Gravy—TAPANULI, NORTH SUMATRA

Tumis Pare
Stir-fried Bitter Gourd —CENTRAL & EAST JAVA

Pacri Nanas
Stir-fried Pineapple in Coconut Milk —SUMATRA

72 *Acar Campur*
Vegetable Pickle

Gohu
Papaya Salad—NORTH SULAWESI

Gedang Mekuah
Papaya and Meat Soup—BALI

Gado-gado
(Mixed Vegetable Salad with Peanut Sauce)
~

50	grams bean sprouts, tailed, blanched, drained
150	grams water convolvulus / morning glory, cut, boiled, drained
150	grams spinach leaves, boiled, drained
200	grams bitter gourd / momordica, seeded, sliced, boiled
1	piece chayote, sliced, boiled
1	piece bean curd (8 x 8 cm), fried, sliced
1	piece fermented soybean (8 x 8 cm), fried, sliced
3	hard-boiled eggs, sliced
1–2	tablespoons fried shallots
	prawn / melinjo nut crackers

Peanut Sauce:

200	grams peanuts, fried, skin removed, ground
2	red chillies, ground
5	bird's eye chillies, ground
1	teaspoon salt, ground
$^1/_2$	tablespoon brown sugar
200	cc water / coconut milk

Peanut Sauce: Mix the sauce ingredients and bring to the boil. ❧ Pour peanut sauce over vegetables, fried bean curd and fermented soybean in a bowl. ❧ Garnish with egg slices, a sprinkle of fried shallots and crushed prawn / melinjo nut crackers.

Note: Do not hesitate to use other vegetables in season, for example sliced carrots, string beans, white cabbage and broccoli.

Rujak Pengantin
(Vegetable Salad with Tangy Peanut Sauce)
~

300	grams potatoes, boiled, cut into wedges
250	grams cucumber, sliced to $^1/_2$ cm thickness
250	grams white cabbage, thinly sliced
200	grams salad leaves, coarsely sliced
2	pieces large bean curd, fried, sliced into pieces 1 x 1 x 3 cm
3	hard-boiled eggs, sliced or quartered
50	grams melinjo nut crackers

Peanut Sauce:

200	grams peanuts, fried and peeled
100	grams dried shrimps, soaked in water, drained
8	red chillies, boiled
2–3	tablespoons vinegar
1	teaspoon salt
3–4	tablespoons sugar
200	cc water

Grind peanuts, dried shrimps and red chillies, and combine with other sauce ingredients. ❧ Arrange the vegetables and fried bean curd on a plate. Pour the sauce over. Garnish with eggs and melinjo nut crackers.

Urap Sayuran
(Mixed Vegetable Salad with Spiced Grated Coconut)
~

100	grams bean sprouts, tailed
4	pieces white cabbage, sliced $^1/_2$ cm thick
100	grams spinach, cut into 2 cm lengths
100	grams string beans, cut into 2 cm lengths
100	grams unripe cassava leaves
$^1/_2$	coconut, peeled and grated

Spices (ground):

3	shallots
2	cloves garlic
1	teaspoon coriander, roasted
$1^1/_2$	teaspoons chopped lesser galangal
3	kaffir lime leaves
1	teaspoon salt
2	teaspoons brown sugar

Blanch the bean sprouts in boiling water for 1 minute, then drain. Boil the white cabbage, spinach, string beans and cassava leaves separately until tender, then drain them. ❧ Mix the vegetables with spiced grated coconut and serve.

Spiced Grated Coconut: Mix the grated coconut with ground spices, and steam for 15 minutes until cooked. Remove and allow to cool.

Note: Do not hesitate to add 25 grams basil leaves and 100 grams Chinese green beans to the vegetables. Or try a combination of 150 grams unripe cassava leaves, 75 grams papaya leaves and 100 grams papaya flowers. 250 grams unripe papaya, grated and steamed, or 250 grams unripe jackfruit, minced and steamed, are also good substitutes.

Opposite: (Clockwise from top) Urap, Rujak Pengantin, Sambal Rujak Pengantin, Gado-gado and Sambal Gado-gado

Keredok

(Fresh Vegetable Salad with Peanut Sauce)
~

100	grams string beans, cut into $1/2$ cm pieces
2	pieces white cabbage, thinly sliced
100	grams bean sprouts, tailed
100	grams round aubergines, cut into 4–8 pieces
100	grams yam bean, cut into 1 cm cubes
100	grams cucumber, peeled, sliced
25	grams basil leaves
50	grams fried crackers

Peanut Sauce:

200	grams peanuts, fried, skin removed
2	red chillies
5	bird's eye chillies
2	teaspoons chopped ginger
$1/2$	teaspoon dried shrimp paste
1–2	tablespoons vinegar
1	teaspoon salt
1	tablespoon brown sugar
150	cc water

Peanut Sauce: Grind all the ingredients and mix well with water.

Mix the vegetables with the peanut sauce, and serve on a plate. Garnish with fried crackers.

Rujak Cingur

(Mixed Vegetable Salad with Black Shrimp Paste Sauce)
~

100	grams bean sprouts, tailed, blanched, drained
100	grams water convolvulus / morning glory, cut, boiled, drained
150	grams string beans, cut to $2^1/2$ cm pieces, boiled, drained
1	piece bean curd, fried, cut into $1^1/2$ cm cubes
200	grams fermented soybean, cut into $1^1/2$ cm cubes, salted, fried, drained
250	grams ox nose, boiled until tender, skinned, fried, cut into 2 cm pieces
1–2	pieces cucumber, thinly sliced
	yam bean, peeled, cut
	prawn crackers

Black Shrimp Paste Sauce:

2	tablespoons peanuts, fried, skin removed
1	unripe banana, sliced
5	bird's eye chillies
1	teaspoon tamarind
2–3	tablespoons black shrimp paste
$1/4$	teaspoon dried shrimp paste
100	cc water
	salt and sugar

Grind and mix the sauce ingredients with water. ❧ Mix the sauce with the cooked vegetables, fried bean curd, fermented soybean, ox nose, cucumber and yam bean. ❧ Serve on a plate and garnish with prawn crackers.

Optional: Serve with *lontong* (rice dumplings).

Opposite: (Clockwise from top) Pecel (page 54),
Keredok and Rujak Cingur

Pecel

(Mixed Vegetable Salad with Spicy Peanut Sauce)

~

150	grams water convolvulus / morning glory, cut into 2 cm pieces
150	grams string beans, cut into 2 cm pieces
150	grams spinach leaves
200	grams bean sprouts, tailed
	salt
3	tablespoons oil

Spicy Peanut Sauce:

6	bird's eye chillies
2	red chillies
1	teaspoon chopped ginger
3	cloves garlic
3	kaffir lime leaves
250	grams peanuts, roasted
1	teaspoon tamarind
	salt and brown sugar
300	cc water

Boil each vegetable separately in water seasoned with salt. Remove after a few minutes and drain.

Sauce: Heat 3 tablespoons oil and sauté chillies, ginger, garlic and kaffir lime leaves until fragrant, then drain. Finely grind with peanuts and other sauce ingredients, add water and stir until the sauce thickens.

Peanut Crackers: Grind 100 grams fried candlenuts, 5 cloves garlic, 2 teaspoons chopped ginger, 1 teaspoon coriander powder and 1 teaspoon salt. ❧ Combine 200 grams rice flour with 50 grams corn starch, ground spices and 1 beaten egg. Mix well, add 450 cc coconut milk, and keep stirring until the mixture becomes smooth. ❧ Then add 5 thinly sliced kaffir lime leaves and 200 grams chopped peanuts. ❧ Take 1 tablespoon of the mixture, and pour it on the side of a frying pan. Let it slide down and harden. Using a wok scoop, put the semi-fried cracker in the centre of the pan and fry over medium heat until golden brown. Turn it over frequently.

Mix the vegetables with the sauce and serve with crushed peanut crackers.

Anyang Pakis

(Ferntop Salad with Roasted Coconut)

~

500	grams ferntops
1/2	shredded coconut, roasted, pounded
5	shallots, thinly sliced
150	grams bean sprouts, tailed, blanched, drained

Spices (ground):

2	tablespoons dried shrimps, roasted
1/2	tablespoon thinly sliced lemon grass
5	red chillies
1	lime, extract the pulp
1/2	teaspoon chopped ginger
	salt and brown sugar

Boil ferntops with a lot of water, then drain. ❧ Mix shredded coconut, ground spices and thinly sliced shallots. ❧ Add the ferntops and bean sprouts. Mix well and serve.

Selada Banjar

(Vegetable Salad with Potato Sauce)

~

350	grams cucumber, peeled, seeded, thinly sliced
150	grams carrots, boiled, thinly sliced
500	grams potatoes, boiled, peeled, thinly sliced
5	hard-boiled eggs, remove yolk, thinly slice the egg white
	lettuce
	fried melinjo nut crackers

Potato Sauce:

100	grams boiled potatoes / potato chips, mashed
5	boiled egg yolks, mashed
1	tablespoon ground fried shallots
1/2	teaspoon pepper
1	tablespoon vinegar / lime juice
2	tablespoons margarine, melted
	salt and sugar

Mix all the ingredients for the sauce and add a dash of salt and sugar to taste. ❧ Arrange the vegetables and egg white slices on a serving dish. Top with the sauce and garnish with melinjo nut crackers.

Opposite: (From left) Anyang Pakis and Selada Banjar

Gulai Buncis
(French Beans Curry)
~

350	grams french beans, thinly sliced
3	tablespoons oil
1	*salam* leaf (or bay leaf as a substitute)
1	stalk lemon grass, bruised
1	piece galangal, bruised
250	grams meat, boiled, cut into 1 cm cubes
350	cc coconut milk from 1/3 coconut
100	grams shredded coconut, roasted, ground
250	grams potatoes, cut into 1 cm cubes

Spices (ground):

3	candlenuts, roasted
1/2	teaspoon chopped turmeric
1	teaspoon chopped ginger
1/4	teaspoon fenugreek
1	teaspoon peppercorns
5	shallots
2	cloves garlic
	salt

Sauté the french beans until tender, drain then set aside. ❧ Heat oil and sauté ground spices, *salam* leaf, lemon grass, and galangal until fragrant. Stir in the meat, coconut milk, and shredded coconut. Bring to the boil, then reduce heat. ❧ Add the sautéed beans and potatoes. Cook until tender.

Gulai Daun Paranci
(Cassava Leaves and Salted Fish Curry)
~

100	grams small salted fish
1	litre thin coconut milk
1	piece dried sour fruit (*Garcinia cambogia*)
1	turmeric leaf
200	grams cassava leaves
500	cc thick coconut milk

Spices (ground):

8	red chillies / 15 bird's eye chillies
1	teaspoon salt
8	shallots
1	teaspoon chopped turmeric
1	teaspoon chopped ginger
1	tablespoon chopped galangal

Grill fish, then wash and drain. ❧ Bring to the boil thin coconut milk. Add ground spices, dried sour fruit, fish and turmeric leaf. Add cassava leaves and cook until the leaves are tender. ❧ Pour in the thick coconut milk and cook over low heat.

Optional: An additional 100 grams string beans, cut into 3 cm pieces.

Gulai Pakis
(Ferntops and Green Beans Curry)
~

750	cc thin coconut milk
1	stalk lemon grass, bruised
1–2	pieces dried sour fruit (*Garcinia cambogia*)
3	kaffir lime leaves
200	grams ferntops
250	grams shrimps, shelled
20	*petai*
250	cc thick coconut milk
	salt

Spices (ground):

10	red chillies
6	shallots
1	teaspoon chopped turmeric
2	teaspoons chopped ginger
3	teaspoons chopped galangal
	salt

Bring to the boil thin coconut milk, then add ground spices, lemon grass, dried sour fruit and kaffir lime leaves. ❧ Add ferntops, shrimps, *petai*, thick coconut milk and salt. Simmer over medium heat.

Opposite: (From left) Gulai Pakis, Gulai Buncis and Gulai Daun Paranci

Gulai Silalab

(Cassava Leaves and Pea Aubergines Curry)

~

1	litre thin coconut milk
50	grams dried shrimps, washed and drained
5	stalks chives
2	teaspoons salt
150	grams cassava leaves
100	grams pea aubergines
3	pink ginger buds
350	cc thick coconut milk

Bring to the boil thin coconut milk, then add dried shrimps, chives and salt. ❧ Pound the cassava leaves and pea aubergines coarsely and add to the boiling milk. Stir, then add pink ginger buds and thick coconut milk. Simmer over medium heat.

Gulai Manis

(Sweet Cabbage Curry)

~

1	litre coconut milk from 1 coconut
6	shallots, thinly sliced
2	cloves garlic, thinly sliced
1	stalk lemon grass, bruised
2	cm galangal, bruised
1	piece *asam gelugur* / dried sour fruit (*Garcinia cambogia*)
2	teaspoons salt
250	grams cabbage / Chinese cabbage, cut into 3 cm pieces
3	red chillies, thinly sliced
2	eggs, lightly beaten

Bring to the boil coconut milk with shallots, garlic, lemon grass, galangal, *asam gelugur* and salt. Add cabbage and chillies, and stir from time to time to prevent the milk from curdling. ❧ Before removing from heat, pour in the eggs quickly, and stir.

Opposite: (From left) Gulai Silalab and Gulai Manis

Sayur Rebung Asam

(Sour Bamboo Shoots Soup)
~

200	grams shrimps / mackerel / snapper / grouper
500	grams sour bamboo shoots
1	stalk lemon grass, bruised
1	piece *asam gelugur*
1	litre coconut milk from 1 coconut
	salt

Spices (ground):

10	red chillies
8	shallots
2	cloves garlic
1	teaspoon powdered ginger
1	tablespoon chopped galangal

Wash shrimps; if using fish, cut into serving pieces. Rub with *asam gelugur*, salt and 2 tablespoons water. Let it stand for 10 minutes. ❧ Put all the ingredients and ground spices into a pan. Bring to the boil, stirring occasionally.

Sour Bamboo Shoots: Thinly slice 500 grams bamboo shoots. Marinate in water or water from washing rice, and leave for 2 days until it tastes sour. Wash and drain.

Sayur Lelawar

(Young Bamboo Shoots in Coconut Milk)
~

500	grams bamboo shoots, sliced into 1 x 1 x 6 cm pieces
750	cc stock
200	grams offal / brisket, boiled, cut into 1 cm cubes
2	*salam* leaves (or bay leaves as a substitute)
500	cc coconut milk from ¹/₂ coconut

Spices (ground):

3	red chillies
3	cloves garlic
7	shallots
¹/₄	teaspoon dried shrimp paste
2	teaspoons coriander
¹/₂	tablespoon chopped galangal
1¹/₂	teaspoons salt
	sugar

Boil the bamboo shoots with 1 tablespoon sugar, then drain. Add fresh water and cook again with fresh water until it does not taste bitter. Remove and drain. ❧ Bring to the boil the stock with the offal / brisket, bamboo shoots, *salam* leaves and ground spices. Stir in the coconut milk, and allow to simmer.

Sayur Gori

(Jackfruit in Coconut Milk)
~

1	kilogram young jackfruit, cut into small pieces
250	grams beef ribs / offal, cook until nearly tender
3	*salam* leaves (or bay leaves as a substitute)
3	cm galangal, bruised
1	litre thin coconut milk
300	cc thick coconut milk
3	red chillies, sliced
3	green chillies, sliced
	salt and sugar

Spices (ground):

2	teaspoons coriander, roasted
¹/₂	teaspoon cumin, roasted
5	candlenuts, roasted
8	shallots
4	cloves garlic
¹/₄	teaspoon dried shrimp paste

Cook jackfruit with ribs / offal, *salam* leaves, galangal and thin coconut milk until tender. ❧ Stir in the ground spices, thick coconut milk, sliced chillies and seasoning. ❧ Stir continuously to prevent the milk from curdling. Simmer until cooked.

Opposite: (From top) Sayur Rebung Asam, Sayur Lelawar and Sayur Gori

Sayur Campur
(Mixed Vegetables in Clear Soup)

8	shallots
4	cloves garlic
1	teaspoon peppercorns
1	tablespoon margarine
5	thin slices galangal
1	stalk lemon grass, bruised
1¼	litres chicken stock
250	grams cooked bamboo shoots, cut into fine strips
3	spring onions, cut into 1 cm pieces
250	grams bean sprouts, tailed
25	grams glass noodles, cut into 10 cm lengths, soaked in water until tender, drained
1	sprig Chinese parsley, chopped

Chicken Croquettes:

150	grams minced chicken
50	grams almonds, ground
1	egg, separate the yolk
¼	teaspoon powdered pepper
1	tablespoon flour
½	teaspoon salt

Grind shallots, garlic and peppercorns. ❧ Heat margarine and sauté ground spices, galangal and lemon grass until fragrant. Add chicken stock, and bring to the boil. Stir in cooked bamboo shoots and spring onions. Then add bean sprouts, glass noodles, chicken croquettes and Chinese parsley.

Chicken Croquettes: Mix all the ingredients thoroughly, leaving out the egg white. Shape the mixture into small balls. Coat each ball with lightly beaten egg white, then toss into boiling water. Remove when the croquettes start to float.

Sayur Lodeh
(Mixed Vegetables in Coconut Milk)

200	grams young jackfruit, cut into small pieces
250	cc thin coconut milk
2	tablespoons dried shrimps, washed and drained
1–2	*salam* leaves (or bay leaves as a substitute)
2	cm galangal, bruised
150	grams string beans, cut into 3 cm pieces
5	green chillies, halved
50	grams melinjo leaves
75	grams fresh melinjo nuts
1	aubergine, halved, then cut into 2–4 pieces
1	litre thick coconut milk
	salt and sugar

Spices (ground):

2	red chillies
3	cloves garlic
7	shallots
½	teaspoon dried shrimp paste
1	teaspoon coriander, roasted
1	teaspoon chopped lesser galangal
1	teaspoon salt

Cook the jackfruit in thin coconut milk until it is tender. Add the ground spices, dried shrimps, *salam* leaves and galangal. ❧ Then add string beans, green chillies, melinjo leaves and nuts, aubergine and thick coconut milk. ❧ Season with salt and sugar, and simmer over low heat, stirring occasionally.

Opposite: (From left) Sayur Campur and Sayur Lodeh

Sayur Brongkos
(French Beans in Black Nut Gravy)

3	tablespoons oil
1	stalk lemon grass
1	piece galangal, bruised
2	kaffir lime leaves
1	*salam* leaf (or bay leaf as a substitute)
1	litre stock
250	grams offal, boiled, cut into 1 cm cubes
50	grams kidney beans, boiled
250	grams french beans, cut into 2 cm pieces
250	cc thick coconut milk

Spices (ground):

1–2	red chillies
1/4	teaspoon cumin
1	teaspoon chopped lesser ginger
1	teaspoon chopped turmeric
3	candlenuts, roasted
1	teaspoon ginger
6	shallots
1	teaspoon tamarind
3	cloves garlic
3	black nuts, soak the pulp with water until tender
2	teaspoons coriander
	salt and sugar

Heat the oil and sauté the ground spices, lemon grass, galangal, kaffir lime leaves and *salam* leaf until fragrant, then pour in the stock. ❧ Add offal, kidney beans and french beans. Stir until tender. Add thick coconut milk, and continue to stir. Simmer until cooked.

Sayur Kare
(Vegetable Curry)

3	tablespoons oil
3	kaffir lime leaves
1	stalk lemon grass, bruised
200	grams offal, cooked until tender, cut into pieces
1	litre stock
250	grams potatoes, peeled, cut into 4–6 pieces
150	grams carrots, halved
100	grams french beans
500	cc coconut milk from 1 coconut
5	cabbage leaves, cut into 2 cm squares
25	grams glass noodles, cut into 10 cm lengths, soaked in water until tender, drained

Spices (ground):

3	candlenuts, roasted
2	teaspoons galangal, minced
2	teaspoons coriander, roasted
2	teaspoons tamarind
1/2	teaspoon pepper, roasted
3	cloves garlic
1	teaspoon chopped turmeric
7	shallots
	salt and sugar

Sauté the ground spices, kaffir lime leaves and lemon grass until fragrant. Add offal and stir. Then add the stock, and simmer over low heat. ❧ Add the potatoes, carrots and french beans. When they are half-cooked, add coconut milk, and bring to the boil. Finally, add cabbage and glass noodles.

Opposite: (Clockwise from top) Sayur Kare, Sayur Podomoro (page 66) and Sayur Brongkos

Sayur Podomoro
(Vegetables and Meat in Spiced Coconut Milk)

150	grams water convolvulus / morning glory
500	cc meat stock
2	salam leaves (or bay leaves as a substitute)
500	cc thin coconut milk
150	grams offal, boiled until tender, cut into pieces
100	grams fermented soybean, cut into 1 cm cubes
100	grams shrimps, shelled
250	cc thick coconut milk from ½ coconut

Spices (ground):
3	candlenuts, roasted
2	teaspoons coriander, roasted
1	teaspoon chopped lesser ginger
½	teaspoon dried shrimp paste
3	cloves garlic
7	shallots
2	red chillies
2	teaspoons chopped galangal
½	teaspoon tamarind
	salt and sugar

Wash water convolvulus and cut into serving pieces. ❧ Pour the stock into a pan and bring to the boil. Add ground spices and salam leaves. Pour in thin coconut milk, and add the offal and fermented soybean. Allow to simmer. ❧ Add shrimps, water convolvulus and thick coconut milk. Simmer until done.

Sayur Bubur
(Spinach in Coconut Milk)

1	litre coconut milk
1	piece galangal, bruised
1	salam leaf (or bay leaf as a substitute)
1	chayote, cut into pieces 1 x 2 cm
150	grams spinach leaves

Spices (ground):
1	teaspoon coriander
1	teaspoon chopped lesser galangal
5	shallots
2	cloves garlic
	salt and sugar

Bring to the boil coconut milk with ground spices, bruised galangal, salam leaf and chayote. ❧ Add the spinach and keep stirring to prevent the coconut milk from curdling. Simmer over low heat.

Ihutilinanga
(Chilli-fried Aubergines in Coconut Milk)

4	aubergines, cut into 6 cm pieces, then halved
3	tablespoons oil
6	shallots, thinly sliced
4	red chillies, thinly sliced
1–2	teaspoons ground red chillies
2	tomatoes, cut
	salt
2	eggs, lightly beaten
200	cc thick coconut milk

Fry aubergines, then drain. Arrange in a serving plate. ❧ Sauté shallots and chillies, then add ground chillies, tomatoes and salt. ❧ Add beaten eggs, stir until the sauce thickens, then pour in the thick coconut milk. Bring to the boil. Pour over the fried aubergines.

Opposite: (From left) Ihutilinanga and Sayur Bubur

Jangan Asem
(Vegetables in Sweet-Sour Gravy)

1	litre stock
300	grams offal, cooked till tender, cut into pieces
5	shallots, sliced
2	cloves garlic, sliced
2	red chillies, sliced coarsely
2	*salam* leaves (or bay leaves as a substitute)
1	piece galangal, bruised
300	grams cucumber, cut into 2–4 pieces
150	grams string beans, cut into 3 cm lengths
1/2	tablespoon tamarind, soaked in water, squeeze the pulp and strain the juice
	salt and sugar

Bring stock to the boil with offal, shallots, garlic, chillies, *salam* leaves and galangal. Add cucumber, string beans, tamarind juice, salt and sugar. Simmer over low heat.

Note: String beans and cucumber can be replaced with water convolvulus / morning glory and soy beans.

Gangan Asam
(Sweet-Sour Vegetable Soup with Fish)

1	catfish (250 grams), washed, cut into 2–3 pieces
1	teaspoon tamarind, soaked in water, squeeze the pulp and strain the juice
	salt
1 1/2	litres water
1	stalk lemon grass, bruised
4	tomatoes, cut into 2–4 pieces
5	green chillies, halved
5	unripe *kepok* bananas, peeled, cut into 3–4 pieces
10	string beans, cut into 3 cm pieces
150	grams water convolvulus / morning glory, cut
5	stalks calladium, about 15 cm long or 5 stalks of lotus flower

Spices (ground):

3	red chillies
1/2	teaspoon dried shrimp paste
3	cloves garlic
7	shallots
1	teaspoon chopped turmeric
1	teaspoon chopped ginger
5	candlenuts, roasted
	salt and sugar

Rub fish with some tamarind juice and salt. Let it stand for 10 minutes. Boil water with ground spices, lemon grass, tomatoes and chillies. Add the fish and *kepok* bananas, and simmer until the ingredients are half-cooked. Add vegetables and simmer until cooked before stirring in the remaining tamarind juice.

Asem-asem Buncis
(French Beans in Sweet-Sour Gravy)

350	grams brisket / offal, cooked until tender
1 1/4	litres meat stock
3	tablespoons oil
4	cloves garlic, sliced
8	shallots, sliced
2	*salam* leaves (or bay leaves as a substitute)
2	pieces galangal, bruised
5	green chillies, cut into big pieces
5	red chillies, cut into big pieces
250	grams french beans, cut into 3 cm pieces
3	slices turmeric
2	slices ginger
5	green tomatoes, quartered
2	red tomatoes, quartered
1	tablespoon tamarind, soaked in 100 cc water, squeeze the pulp and strain the juice
1–2	tablespoons sweet soy sauce
1	tablespoon salt
1	tablespoon sugar

Cut meat into 1 cm cubes and add to the stock. Heat oil and sauté garlic, shallots, *salam* leaves and galangal. Then add red and green chillies and french beans. Add turmeric and ginger, and simmer over low heat. Add tomatoes, tamarind juice, sweet soy sauce, salt and sugar. Simmer until cooked.

Opposite: (From left) Jangan Asem, Asem-asem Buncis and Gangan Asam

Tumis Kacang Panjang
(Stir-fried String Beans in Coconut Gravy)
~

3	tablespoons oil
7	shallots, thinly sliced
5	red chillies, cut into large pieces
1	stalk lemon grass, bruised
5	chicken gizzards, boiled, thinly sliced
150	grams shrimps, shelled
250	grams string beans, cut diagonally
500	cc coconut milk from 1 coconut
1	piece *asam gelugur*
	salt and sugar

Spices (ground):

1	tablespoon galangal
2	teaspoons chopped turmeric
2	teaspoons ginger
3	cloves garlic

Heat oil and sauté shallots and chillies until soft, then add ground spices and lemon grass. Cook until fragrant. Add chicken gizzards, shrimps and string beans. Cook until tender, then pour in the coconut milk and add the *asam gelugur*. Season with salt and sugar. ❧ Cook until the gravy thickens.

Note: String beans can be replaced with french beans.

Tumis Pare
(Stir-fried Bitter Gourd)
~

500	grams bitter gourd / momordica
1	tablespoon salt
3	tablespoons oil
1	*salam* leaf (or bay leaf as a substitute)
1	piece galangal, bruised
150	grams shrimps, shelled
	salt and sugar

Spices (ground):

5	red chillies
1	tomato
3	candlenuts, roasted
2	teaspoons salt
3	cloves garlic
1/2	teaspoon dried shrimp paste
7	shallots

Cut the bitter gourd into two, and scoop out the seeds. Cut into 1/2 cm pieces. Then squeeze the bitter gourd with 1 tablespoon salt until tender and foamy to reduce the bitter taste. Wash and drain. ❧ Heat oil and sauté ground spices, *salam* leaf and galangal until fragrant, then add bitter gourd and shrimps. Pour in 100 cc water, and add salt and sugar. Cook until the gravy is completely absorbed.

Pacri Nanas
(Stir-fried Pineapple in Coconut Milk)
~

3	tablespoons oil
2	cloves garlic, sliced
6	shallots, sliced
1	pineapple, cut into 1 cm thick slices
5	cm cinnamon
1	star anise
4	cloves
2–3	cardamoms, bruised
300	cc coconut milk from 1/2 coconut
125	grams brown sugar
5	green chillies, coarsely sliced
5	red chillies, coarsely sliced

Spices (ground):

3	red chillies
1/4	teaspoon cumin
1/4	teaspoon aniseed
2	cloves garlic
5	shallots
1/2	teaspoon chopped turmeric
1	teaspoon salt

Heat oil and sauté the garlic and shallots until fragrant. Add the ground spices and stir until fragrant. Then add pineapple and other spices. ❧ When the pineapple is half-cooked, add coconut milk, sugar and red and green chillies. Simmer over low heat.

Opposite: (From left) Tumis Kacang Panjang and Tumis Pare

Acar Campur
(Vegetable Pickle)
~

300	grams cucumber
150	grams carrots
150	grams bamboo shoots
3	tablespoons oil
1	stalk lemon grass, bruised
1	pandanus leaf, cut into 5 cm pieces
250	cc water
1–2	teaspoons vinegar
100	grams french beans, cut into 3 cm pieces, then slit lengthwise
100	grams peanuts, boiled and skinned
10	bird's eye chillies
1–2	tablespoons sugar

Spices (ground):

5	candlenuts, roasted
1	teaspoon chopped turmeric
2	cloves garlic
4	shallots
1	teaspoon salt

Cut the cucumber, carrots and bamboo shoots into 1 x 1 x 3 cm pieces. Boil bamboo shoots to remove bitterness. ❧ Heat oil and sauté ground spices, lemon grass and pandanus leaf until fragrant. Add water and vinegar, and bring to the boil. ❧ Add cooked bamboo shoots, french beans, carrots, cucumber, peanuts and bird's eye chillies. Add sugar to taste. Remove from heat when ingredients are cooked thoroughly.

Gohu
(Papaya Salad)
~

500	grams young papaya, cut ½ x ½ x 2 cm
500	cc palm vinegar or 500 cc water with 1–2 tablespoons vinegar
1	teaspoon salt
	sugar

Spices (ground):

5	red chillies / bird's eye chillies
2	teaspoons chopped ginger

Mix the ground spices, vinegar, salt and sugar. ❧ Add the papaya, stir and keep for 2–3 hours before serving.

Gedang Mekuah
(Papaya and Meat Soup)
~

3	tablespoons oil
2	*salam* leaves (or bay leaves as a substitute)
2	stalks lemon grass, bruised
2	kaffir lime leaves
500	grams young papaya, cut 1 x 2 x 3 cm
200	grams offal, cooked and cut into cubes
750	cc stock
	fried shallots

Spices (ground):

3	red chillies
5	bird's eye chillies
1	teaspoon chopped lesser galangal
1	tablespoon chopped galangal
1	teaspoon chopped turmeric
½	teaspoon peppercorns
1	teaspoon coriander, roasted
3	candlenuts, roasted
½	teaspoon dried shrimp paste
½	teaspoon tamarind
6	shallots
3	cloves garlic
	salt and sugar

Heat oil and sauté the ground spices, *salam* leaves, lemon grass and kaffir lime leaves until fragrant. Add papaya and offal, and stir until soft. Pour in the stock. ❧ Simmer over low heat until cooked. Serve with a sprinkle of fried shallots.

Note: Young papaya can be replaced with chayote or vegetable marrow.

Top: (From left) Gohu and Gedang Mekuah.
Opposite: (From left) Acar Campur and Pacri Nanas (page 70)

POULTRY

Soto Banjar
(Chicken and Vermicelli Soup)
~

1	chicken, cut into 2–4 pieces
2	litres water
1/2	nutmeg
5	cm cinnamon stick
4	cloves
2	cardamoms
100	grams shallots
5	cloves garlic
1	tablespoon margarine
1/2	teaspoon pepper
1	ketupat (5 x 5 cm), cut into cubes
100	grams vermicelli (glass noodles), soaked until tender, drained, cut
3–4	spring onions, finely sliced
2	sprigs Chinese parsley, finely chopped
3	hard-boiled eggs, quartered
	potato croquettes
2	tablespoons fried shallots
	sweet soy sauce and lime

Sambal:

50	grams red chillies
10	bird's eye chillies
5	candlenuts, roasted
1	teaspoon dried shrimp paste
	salt and sugar
1	tablespoon oil

Boil the chicken in 2 litres water until tender, drain, and shred meat when cool. Reserve 1 1/2 litres stock. Wrap nutmeg, cinnamon, cloves and cardamoms in a small piece of cloth. ❧ Grind shallots and garlic until fine. Heat the margarine and sauté ground shallots and garlic until fragrant. Add wrapped spices and pepper. ❧ Put the sautéed spices into the stock. Cover the saucepan, and continue to simmer for about 30 minutes. Season to taste, and serve hot.

Sambal: Grind all the ingredients except oil. Heat oil and sauté the ground ingredients until fragrant and crispy.

How to serve: Arrange ketupat (compressed rice cakes), glass noodles, shredded chicken, spring onions and parsley in a bowl. Add a few pieces of egg and potato croquette. Pour boiling chicken stock over and garnish with fried shallots. Serve with sambal, soy sauce and lime.

Potato Croquettes: Mash 350 grams boiled potatoes, and add 1/4 teaspoon salt, 1/4 teaspoon pepper, 1/8 teaspoon grated nutmeg, and 1 egg yolk. Shape into 4–5 balls. Dip the potato balls in beaten egg white, and fry until golden brown.

Soto Kudus
(Clear Chicken Soup)
~

1	chicken, cut into 2–4 pieces
2	litres water
2	tablespoons oil
8	shallots, ground
4	cloves garlic, ground
2	salam leaves (or bay leaves as a substitute)
1	piece galangal, bruised
	oil for deep-frying
	salt
1/2	teaspoon pepper
3–4	tablespoons sweet soy sauce
200	grams bean sprouts, tailed, blanched, drained
3	sprigs Chinese parsley, finely chopped
10	stalks chives, cut into 2 cm pieces
3	spring onions, finely chopped
3–4	tablespoons fried shallots, crushed
3	tablespoons finely sliced garlic, fried, crushed
1–2	limes, extract the juice

Boil the chicken pieces in 2 litres water. ❧ Heat oil and sauté ground shallots and garlic until soft. Add to the stock together with salam leaves and galangal. Continue to cook over low heat until the chicken is tender. ❧ Remove chicken, reserving 1 1/2 litres stock. Drain, then deep-fry the chicken until golden brown. ❧ Bring chicken stock to the boil, then add salt, pepper and sweet soy sauce.

How to serve: Arrange bean sprouts, shredded chicken, Chinese parsley, chives, spring onion, fried shallots and garlic in a bowl, then pour the stock over. Serve with bird's eye chillies, sambal and lime juice.

Opposite: (Clockwise from top) Soto Banjar, Soto Ayam Bersantan (page 78), Soto Kudus and Soto Ayam Madura (page 78)

Soto Ayam Madura
(Chicken and Bean Sprouts Soup)
~

1	chicken, cut into 2–4 pieces
2	litres water
	oil for deep-frying
3	tablespoons oil
1	stalk lemon grass, bruised
3	kaffir lime leaves
50	grams glass noodles, cut, soaked in water until tender, drained
100	grams short bean sprouts, blanched, drained
3	spring onions, chopped
2	sprigs Chinese parsley, chopped
1–2	tablespoons fried shallots
75	grams potato chips
4	hard-boiled eggs, quartered
	sweet soy sauce and lime juice

Spices (ground):

1	teaspoon chopped ginger
2	teaspoons chopped turmeric
1	teaspoon peppercorns
4	candlenuts roasted / fried
5	cloves garlic
1	teaspoon salt

Boil chicken in water until tender. Remove chicken, reserving 1¹/₂ litres stock. Deep-fry the chicken until crispy, then shred finely. ❧ Heat 3 tablespoons oil and sauté ground spices, lemon grass and kaffir lime leaves until fragrant, then add the stock. Continue to simmer over low heat for about 30 minutes.

Sambal Soto: Boil 5 red chillies and 5 bird's eye chillies, drain, and grind with salt.

How to serve: Arrange glass noodles, bean sprouts, chicken, spring onions, Chinese parsley and fried shallots in a bowl, and pour boiling stock over. Garnish with potato chips and egg. Serve with *sambal*, sweet soy sauce and lime juice.

Soto Ayam Bersantan
(Rich Chicken Soup)
~

3	tablespoons oil
3	stalks lemon grass, bruised
5	kaffir lime leaves
2	*salam* leaves (or bay leaves as a substitute)
2	cm galangal, bruised
1	chicken, cut into 2–4 pieces
1	litre thin coconut milk
	salt
	oil for deep-frying
250	cc thick coconut milk

Spices (ground):

3	tablespoons coriander, roasted
1	teaspoon cumin, roasted
1	teaspoon peppercorns
3	cloves garlic
7	shallots
1	teaspoon chopped ginger
1	teaspoon chopped turmeric
	salt

Garnishing:

350	grams boiled potatoes, sliced
250	grams tomatoes, finely sliced
5	hard-boiled eggs, quartered
100	grams fried melinjo nut crackers
2–3	tablespoons fried shallots
10	red chillies, ground for *sambal*
	finely sliced lime and sweet soy sauce

Heat oil and sauté ground spices, lemon grass, kaffir lime and *salam* leaves and galangal until fragrant. Add chicken. Stir, then pour in thin coconut milk. Allow to simmer until the chicken is tender. ❧ Remove the chicken, rub with salt, and deep-fry until golden brown. Remove from oil and drain. Shred the chicken meat finely, then set aside. ❧ Pour thick coconut milk into the gravy, and bring to the boil.

How to serve: Arrange chicken, potatoes, tomatoes, egg quarters and melinjo nut crackers in a bowl, and pour the hot gravy over. Sprinkle with fried shallots, and add *sambal*, sliced lime and sweet soy sauce. Serve with rice or *ketupat* (compressed rice cakes).

Opposite: Ayam Goreng Lengkuas (page 80)

Ayam Goreng Lengkuas
(Galangal-fried Chicken)
~

1	chicken (weighing about 1 kg), cut into 8 pieces
4	tablespoons shredded galangal
5	tablespoons oil
2	*salam* leaves (or bay leaves as a substitute)
1	stalk lemon grass, bruised
	oil for deep-frying

Spices (ground):

3	cloves garlic
5	shallots
3	candlenuts, roasted
1	teaspoon tamarind
2	teaspoons chopped turmeric
	salt and sugar

Combine chicken with ground spices and shredded galangal and mix thoroughly. ❧ Heat oil in a frying pan and fry the chicken. Add *salam* leaves and lemon grass. Cover the pan and fry over low heat, adding a little water if necessary. Remove the chicken when it is half-cooked. ❧ Deep-fry the chicken until golden brown, then drain. Serve the chicken with fried shredded galangal sprinkled on it.

Ayam Goreng Balado
(Chilli-fried Chicken)
~

100	grams red chillies
1½	teaspoons salt
1	chicken, cut into 8–10 pieces
1	tablespoon tamarind / lime juice
	oil for deep-frying
6	tablespoons oil
8	shallots, thinly sliced
1	tomato, chopped
1–2	tablespoons lime juice

Pound chillies coarsely with 1 teaspoon salt. ❧ Rub chicken with ½ teaspoon salt and tamarind juice. Knead gently. ❧ Deep-fry chicken over medium heat until golden brown. Drain. ❧ Heat 6 tablespoons oil and sauté shallots, then add pounded chillies and chopped tomato (add a dash of sugar to reduce the pungent smell). Keep stirring until ingredients are cooked. ❧ Toss in the fried chicken, mix well, then add lime juice.

Ayam Tuturaga
(Fragrant Curried Chicken, Manado-style)
~

1	chicken (weighing 1 kg), cut
½	teaspoon salt
1	tablespoon lime juice
5	tablespoons oil
2	pandanus leaves, cut into 2 cm pieces
2	stalks lemon grass, finely chopped
5	kaffir lime leaves
2	cumin leaves, coarsely chopped
2	eggs, lightly beaten
250	cc water
4–5	stalks chives, cut into 2 cm pieces
1–2	tablespoons lime juice
	salt and sugar

Spices (ground):

100	grams red and bird's eye chillies
5	cloves garlic
10	shallots
2	teaspoons chopped ginger
2	teaspoons chopped turmeric
7	candlenuts, roasted
1	teaspoon salt

Rub chicken with salt and lime juice, and let it stand for 15 minutes. ❧ Heat oil and sauté ground spices, pandanus leaves, lemon grass, kaffir lime and cumin leaves until fragrant. ❧ Add chicken and fry until it is half-cooked. Add beaten eggs, stir until the eggs are cooked, then add water. Continue to cook until the chicken is tender and the gravy has thickened. Add chives, lime juice, and salt and sugar to taste.

Note: This dish originally used turtle meat. To make our dish resemble the original one, we added the lightly beaten eggs.

Opposite: (From left) Ayam Tuturaga and Ayam Goreng Balado

Ayam Panggang Bumbu Kuning
(Yellow Spiced Grilled Chicken)

3	tablespoons oil
1	stalk lemon grass, bruised
3	kaffir lime leaves
2	cloves
2	cardamoms, bruised
1	chicken, cut into 2–4 pieces
500	cc thick coconut milk
1	piece *asam gelugur* or 1 tablespoon tamarind juice

Spices (ground):

3	teaspoons coriander
1	teaspoon pepper
1/2	teaspoon cumin
1/4	teaspoon aniseed
1/4	teaspoon nutmeg
2	teaspoons chopped ginger
2	teaspoons chopped turmeric
1/4	teaspoon chopped galangal
5	candlenuts, roasted
4	cloves garlic
8	shallots
1	tablespoon salt

Heat oil and sauté the ground spices, lemon grass, kaffir lime leaves, cloves and cardamoms until fragrant. Add the chicken. Fry for a few minutes, then add coconut milk and *asam gelugur* or tamarind juice. ❧ Simmer until the chicken is half-cooked and the sauce has reduced. Remove the chicken from the sauce. ❧ Grill the chicken over hot charcoal, brushing it with some sauce. ❧ Serve with the remaining sauce.

Ayam Panggang Bumbu Rujak
(Grilled Chicken with Sour Sauce)

1	chicken, cut into 2–4 pieces
1/2	teaspoon tamarind, soaked in water, squeeze the pulp and strain the juice
3	tablespoons oil
1–2	*salam* leaves (or bay leaves as a substitute)
1	stalk lemon grass, bruised
500	cc coconut milk from 1 coconut

Spices (ground):

10	red chillies
4	cloves garlic
8	shallots
5	candlenuts, roasted
1	teaspoon chopped ginger
1/2	teaspoon tamarind
1	tablespoon salt
	brown sugar

Rub chicken with tamarind juice and let it stand for 10 minutes. ❧ Heat oil and sauté ground spices, *salam* leaves and lemon grass until fragrant. Add chicken, then pour in the coconut milk. Continue to cook until the chicken is tender and the sauce has thickened. ❧ Remove the chicken and grill over hot charcoal or in an oven, brushing it with sautéed spices. Cut into small pieces before serving.

Opposite: (Clockwise from top) Ayam Panggang Bumbu Kuning, Ayam Panggang Bumbu Rujak and Ayam Panggang Kecap (page 84)

Ayam Panggang Kecap
(Grilled Chicken with Sweet Soy Sauce)
~

1	chicken, cut into 2–4 pieces
1	teaspoon tamarind
1	teaspoon salt
3	tablespoons oil
250	cc water
6	tablespoons sweet soy sauce
1	lime, extract juice

Spices (ground):

2	red chillies
8	shallots
4	cloves garlic
1	teaspoon peppercorns
3	candlenuts, fried
3–4	tablespoons sweet soy sauce
1	teaspoon salt
	sugar

Rub chicken with tamarind and salt mixed with 2 tablespoons of water. ❧ Heat oil and sauté ground spices until fragrant. Add chicken, then pour in 250 cc water and sweet soy sauce. When the chicken is half-cooked and the sauce has thickened, add lime juice. Set aside. ❧ Grill the chicken over hot charcoal, brushing it with the sautéed spices. Cut before serving.

Ayam Rica-Rica
(Hot and Spicy Grilled Chicken)
~

1	chicken (weighing 1 kg), cut into 4 pieces
1	teaspoon salt
1–2	tablespoons lime juice
5	tablespoons oil
	salt

Spices (ground):

100	grams red chillies
25	grams red bird's eye chillies
6	shallots
5	cloves garlic
1/2	teaspoon dried shrimp paste
3	teaspoons chopped ginger
2–3	tomatoes, chopped
1/2	teaspoon salt

Rub chicken with 1 teaspoon salt and lime juice, and let it stand for 15 minutes. ❧ Heat oil and gently fry ground spices until fragrant and season with salt. Add chicken and cook for a few minutes. Add a little water and simmer until the chicken is half-cooked. Remove the chicken, and allow to cool. ❧ Grill chicken pieces over hot charcoal or in an oven, turning them over from time to time. Brush with the remaining sauce.

Ayam Masak di Belanga
(Spicy Clay Pot Chicken)
~

1	chicken, cut into small pieces
1	teaspoon salt
1–2	tablespoons lime juice
3	tablespoons oil
1/2	turmeric leaf, finely sliced
1	pandanus leaf, finely sliced
3	kaffir lime leaves, finely sliced
2	stalks lemon grass, bruised
4	green chillies, coarsely sliced
2	spring onions, cut into 2 cm pieces
25	grams basil leaves

Spices (ground):

7	red chillies
2	teaspoons turmeric
2	teaspoons ginger
7	shallots
3	cloves garlic
2	chopped tomatoes
1	tablespoon salt

Rub chicken with 1 teaspoon salt and lime juice, and let it stand for 10 minutes. ❧ Heat oil and sauté the ground spices until fragrant. Add the chicken, turmeric leaf, pandanus leaf, kaffir lime leaves and lemon grass. Fry for a few minutes before adding enough water to cover the chicken. Bring to the boil. ❧ Simmer until the chicken is tender, then add green chillies, spring onions and basil leaves. Cook until the gravy thickens.

Opposite: (From left) Ayam Masak di Belanga and Ayam Rica-Rica

Ayam Masak Habang
(Fried Chicken in Spicy Tomato Sauce)
~

1	chicken (weighing 1 kg), cut into serving pieces
1	teaspoon tamarind
1	teaspoon salt
	oil for deep-frying
3	tablespoons oil
1	stalk lemon grass, bruised
2	tomatoes, finely chopped
350	cc water

Spices (ground):

8	red chillies
6	shallots
3	cloves garlic
4	candlenuts, fried
1	teaspoon chopped lesser galangal
1	teaspoon chopped ginger
2	teaspoons chopped galangal
1–2	tablespoons tamarind juice
1/2	teaspoon dried shrimp paste
	salt and sugar

Rub chicken with tamarind and salt mixed with 2 tablespoons water, and let it stand for 15 minutes. Deep-fry chicken until golden brown. ❧ Heat 3 tablespoons oil and sauté the ground spices until fragrant. Add lemon grass, tomatoes and water, and bring to the boil. ❧ Add the fried chicken, and cook until it is tender and the gravy has thickened.

Ayam Betutu
(Grilled Chicken)
~

5	tablespoons oil
100	grams young cassava leaves, boiled until tender, cut into serving pieces
1	chicken (weighing 1 1/2 kg)
	banana leaves / aluminium foil, for wrapping

Spices (ground):

7	red chillies
5	bird's eye chillies
5	candlenuts, roasted
10	shallots
1	teaspoon dried shrimp paste
5	cloves garlic
1	tablespoon coriander, roasted
1 1/2	tablespoons sliced lemon grass
2	teaspoons peppercorns
1	tablespoon chopped galangal
1/2	teaspoon powdered nutmeg
2	teaspoons chopped turmeric
4	kaffir lime leaves
2	teaspoons chopped ginger
2	teaspoons chopped lesser galangal
	salt and sugar

Heat oil and sauté the ground spices until fragrant and dry. Set aside and allow to cool. Divide into 2 parts. ❧ Combine 1 part with cassava leaves. Stuff the mixture into the chicken and secure with toothpicks. Rub the chicken with the remaining ground spices. ❧ Wrap the chicken with banana leaves and tie with a string. Grill in the oven at medium heat (180°C) for 2–3 hours or until cooked. ❧ Remove from heat and cut before serving.

Note: Another way to cook the chicken is to steam it for about 45 minutes before grilling in the oven for 1 hour.
Betutu is a special dish from Bali. Usually the Balinese use duck wrapped in banana leaves, and wrapped again with stalks of palm leaves. The duck is then buried in the ground and covered with hot charcoal for 6–7 hours until cooked.

Opposite: (From top) Ayam Betutu and Ayam Masak Habang

Garang Asem
(Chicken in Sweet-Sour Soup)

1	tablespoon margarine / 3 tablespoons oil
1	stalk lemon grass, bruised
4	slices turmeric
1/2	chicken, cut into 6 pieces
1 1/2	litres water
6	cabbage leaves, cut into 5 x 5 cm pieces

Spices (ground):
2	red chillies
1	teaspoon coriander, roasted
1/4	teaspoon cumin, roasted
3	candlenuts, roasted
1/4	teaspoon dried shrimp paste
6	shallots
3	cloves garlic
2	teaspoon tamarind
	salt and sugar

Heat margarine or oil and sauté ground spices, lemon grass and turmeric until fragrant. ❧ Boil chicken with 1 1/2 litres water until tender. Add sautéed spices. Continue to cook over low heat for 15 minutes, then add cabbage. Boil for 5 minutes.

Pencok Ayam
(Grilled Chicken in Spicy Coconut Gravy)

1	young chicken, cut into 2 pieces
1	tablespoon tamarind juice
1	teaspoon salt
350	cc coconut milk from 1/2 coconut
25	grams basil leaves

Spices (ground):
5	red chillies
4	shallots
2	cloves garlic
5	candlenuts, fried
1/2	teaspoon peppercorns
1	teaspoon chopped lesser galangal
1/2	teaspoon tamarind
	salt and sugar

Rub chicken with tamarind juice and 1 teaspoon salt, and let it stand for 10 minutes. ❧ Grill chicken over hot charcoal or in an oven until golden brown. ❧ Shred chicken meat and arrange in a bowl. ❧ Bring to the boil coconut milk with ground spices, then pour gravy over shredded chicken. Garnish with basil leaves.

Opor Manuk
(Chicken in Spiced Coconut Milk)

1	chicken, cut into 8 pieces
1	litre coconut milk from 1 coconut
3	tablespoons oil
2	cloves
5	cm cinnamon stick

Spices (ground):
8	red chillies
2	teaspoons coriander, roasted
1/4	teaspoon cumin, roasted
1	teaspoon black pepper
4	candlenuts, roasted
1	tablespoon chopped galangal
1/2	teaspoon chopped lesser galangal
1/2	teaspoon chopped ginger
8	shallots
4	cloves garlic
	salt and sugar

Boil chicken in coconut milk until half-cooked, stirring from time to time to prevent the milk from curdling. ❧ Heat oil and sauté ground spices, cloves and cinnamon until fragrant, then add to the chicken. Simmer until chicken is cooked.

Opposite: (From left) Pencok Ayam and Garang Asem

Opor Ayam
(Chicken in Coconut Milk)
~

1	chicken, cut into 8 pieces
1	tablespoon tamarind juice
1	teaspoon salt
3	tablespoons oil
1	stalk lemon grass, bruised
3	kaffir lime leaves
1	*salam* leaf (or bay leaf as a substitute)
750	cc thin coconut milk
250	cc thick coconut milk
	fried shallots

Spices (ground):

4	cloves garlic
7	shallots
4	candlenuts, roasted
1	teaspoon powdered coriander
1/2	teaspoon powdered cumin
1/2	teaspoon powdered pepper
1/2	tablespoon chopped ginger
1	tablespoon chopped galangal
	salt and sugar

Rub chicken with 1 tablespoon tamarind juice and 1 teaspoon salt, and let it stand for 25 minutes. Rinse and drain. ❧ Heat oil and gently fry ground spices, lemon grass, kaffir lime leaves and *salam* leaf until fragrant. ❧ Add chicken, cook for a few minutes, then pour in thin coconut milk. Bring to the boil. After the chicken is half-cooked, pour in thick coconut milk. ❧ Simmer over low heat until the ingredients are cooked. Season with salt and sugar to taste. Sprinkle with fried shallots and serve.

Gulai Ayam
(Chicken in Chilli Gravy)
~

3	tablespoons oil
1	stalk lemon grass, bruised
3	kaffir lime leaves
3	cm cinnamon stick
2	cloves
1/2	nutmeg
2	cardamoms, bruised
1	chicken (1 kg), cut into 8 pieces
50	grams shredded coconut, roasted, pounded
1	litre coconut milk from 3/4 coconut
1	piece *asam gelugur* or 1 tablespoon tamarind juice

Spices (ground):

10	red chillies
1	teaspoon peppercorns
1	tablespoon coriander, roasted
1/2	teaspoon cumin, roasted
1/4	teaspoon aniseed
2	teaspoons chopped turmeric
2	teaspoons chopped ginger
1	tablespoon chopped galangal
4	cloves garlic
8	shallots
	salt

Heat oil and sauté ground spices with lemon grass, kaffir lime leaves, cinnamon, cloves, nutmeg and cardamoms until fragrant. Add the chicken pieces. ❧ Add shredded coconut and mix well. Then pour in coconut milk and *asam gelugur*. ❧ Cook until the chicken is tender and the gravy has thickened. If you prefer, add 300 grams peeled and quartered potatoes to the gravy along with the chicken.

Opposite: (Clockwise from top) Opor Manuk (page 88), Gulai Ayam and Opor Ayam

Pais Ayam
(Grilled Chicken in Banana Leaf)
~

1	chicken, cut into 8 pieces
1	teaspoon tamarind
	salt
2	tablespoons oil
6–7	*salam* leaves (or bay leaves as a substitute)
3–4	stalks lemon grass, halved, bruised
350	cc coconut milk from 1 coconut
	banana leaves, for wrapping

Spices (ground):

8	candlenuts, roasted / fried
1/2	tablespoon chopped galangal
1	teaspoon chopped turmeric
6	shallots
3	cloves garlic
1	teaspoon coriander
1/4	teaspoon powdered cumin
1/2	teaspoon pepper
	salt and sugar

Rub chicken with tamarind and salt. Set aside. ↩* Heat oil and sauté ground spices, *salam* leaves and lemon grass until fragrant. Add the chicken and fry for a few minutes. Pour in coconut milk, stirring from time to time until the chicken is half-cooked. ↩* Take 1–2 pieces banana leaf and add 1 salam leaf and 1 stalk lemon grass. Place 3–4 pieces chicken. Roll up and secure both ends with toothpicks. Repeat for the rest of the chicken. ↩* Grill chicken until it is cooked and dry.

Kari Ayam
(Chicken Curry)
~

1	chicken, cut into 8 pieces
1	tablespoon lime juice / tamarind juice
1	teaspoon salt
3	tablespoons oil
3	shallots, finely sliced
3	cm cinnamon stick
1	star anise
2	cloves
2	cardamoms
1	stalk lemon grass, bruised
1–2	pandanus leaves, shredded, knotted
5	curry leaves
500	cc coconut milk from 1 1/2 coconuts
3	tablespoons roasted shredded coconut, pounded

Spices (ground):

3	candlenuts, roasted
1	tablespoon coriander
1	teaspoon cumin, roasted
1	teaspoon aniseed
1/8	nutmeg
10	red chillies
6	shallots
3	cloves garlic
1	teaspoon chopped turmeric
2	teaspoons chopped ginger
1	tablespoon salt

Rub chicken with lime or tamarind juice and salt, and let it stand for 15 minutes. ↩* Heat oil and sauté shallots until golden brown, then add ground spices, whole spices, lemon grass, pandanus leaves, curry leaves and chicken. Cook for a few minutes, then add coconut milk and pounded coconut. ↩* Continue to cook, stirring from time to time until the chicken is cooked and the gravy is thick and oily. ↩* Serve with cane bread or lacy pancakes.

Opposite: (From left) Pais Ayam and Kari Ayam

Kalio Ayam
(Chicken Stewed in Coconut Milk)
~

750	cc coconut milk from 1 coconut
1	turmeric leaf, shredded, tied
1	stalk lemon grass, bruised
3	kaffir lime leaves
1	piece *asam gelugur* or
1/2	tablespoon tamarind juice
1	chicken, cut into 8 pieces

Spices (ground):

100	grams red chillies
1 1/2	tablespoons chopped galangal
2	teaspoons chopped turmeric
2	teaspoons chopped ginger
8	shallots
1	teaspoon powdered coriander
1	tablespoon salt

Simmer coconut milk with ground spices, turmeric leaf, lemon grass, kaffir lime leaves and *asam gelugur*. Keep stirring until the milk becomes oily. ~ Add chicken and simmer until it is cooked and the gravy has thickened. Serve.

Botok Jerohan
(Chicken Innards in Banana Leaf)
~

6	chicken gizzards
6	chicken hearts
6	chicken livers
200	grams chicken intestines, cleaned, cut into 5 cm pieces
2–3	stalks lemon grass, bruised, cut into 7 cm pieces
6–7	*salam* leaves (or bay leaves as a substitute)
15	bird's eye chillies
4	red chillies, slit lengthwise
10	carambolas, sliced
350	cc coconut milk from 1/2 coconut banana leaves, for wrapping

Spices (ground):

5	shallots
2	cloves garlic
2	teaspoons galangal
1	teaspoon lesser galangal
2	candlenuts, roasted
1/2	teaspoon dried shrimp paste
1/2	tablespoon salt
1	tablespoon brown sugar

Mix ground spices with innards. ~ Take 2 banana leaves, and put 1 piece lemon grass, 1 *salam* leaf, 1/8 of the innards mixture, bird's eye chillies, red chillies, carambola slices and 1/8 of the coconut milk. ~ Wrap banana leaf in the shape of a pyramid. Steam for 45 minutes until cooked. Remove from heat and serve.

Ungkep Jerohan
(Spicy Chicken Innards)
~

10	chicken gizzards
10	chicken livers
10	chicken intestines, 20 cm long
2	*salam* leaves (or bay leaves as a substitute)
5	tablespoons oil

Spices (ground):

4	cloves garlic
4	shallots
1	tablespoon finely chopped galangal
1	teaspoon tamarind
3	candlenuts, roasted
	salt and sugar

Clean innards and drain. Use chicken intestines to wrap up gizzards and livers, then secure with toothpicks. ~ Put the innards with ground spices, *salam* leaves and water in a frying pan. Simmer over low heat until the water has evaporated and the innards are tender. ~ Add oil and fry until the innards becomes golden brown. Remove from heat and serve.

Opposite: (Clockwise from top) Ungkep Jerohan,
Botok Jerohan and Kalio Ayam

Semur Ayam
(Fried Chicken in Soy Sauce Gravy)

1	chicken, cut into 8 pieces
1	tablespoon tamarind juice
1	teaspoon salt
	oil for deep-frying
4	cloves garlic
1	teaspoon chopped ginger
1	tablespoon margarine
7	shallots, finely sliced
4–5	tablespoons sweet soy sauce
1–2	tomatoes, chopped coarsely
3	cm cinnamon stick
1/4	nutmeg, bruised
2	cloves
1/2	teaspoon pepper
500	cc chicken stock
300	grams peeled potatoes, cut into 4–6 pieces, fried, drained
25	grams glass noodles, soaked in water until tender, cut into 10 cm lengths
	fried shallots

Rub chicken with tamarind juice and salt. Let it stand for 10 minutes, then deep-fry until golden brown. ❧ Grind garlic and ginger. Heat margarine and sauté shallots until soft, then add ground garlic and ginger, sweet soy sauce and chopped tomato. Sauté until fragrant. Add cinnamon, nutmeg, cloves, pepper and chicken stock, and bring to the boil. When the gravy is boiling, add fried chicken. Simmer until the chicken is tender and the spices are absorbed. ❧ Add fried potatoes and glass noodles, and continue to cook. Garnish with fried shallots.

Sop Ayam
(Chicken Soup)

1	chicken (old chicken, if available), cut into serving pieces
2	litres water
1	tablespoon margarine
5	shallots, finely sliced, fried
1/4	nutmeg, bruised
2	cloves
1/2	teaspoon pepper
2	cloves garlic, finely chopped
200	grams potatoes, peeled, cut into 1 1/2 cm cubes
150	grams carrots, sliced, shaped into flowers
2	spring onions, cut into small pieces
1	sprig Chinese parsley, knotted
4	cabbage leaves, cut 2 x 2 cm
50	grams snow peas, cut both ends
100	grams frozen / fresh peas
1	tablespoon flour, mixed with a little water
	salt
	fried shallots

Simmer chicken in a covered pot until tender. Remove chicken and separate meat from the bones. Cut the chicken meat into 1 cm cubes. ❧ Heat margarine and sauté shallots, nutmeg, cloves, pepper and garlic. Add to the boiling stock. ❧ Add potatoes, carrots, spring onions and Chinese parsley. Just before removing from heat, add cabbage, snow peas, peas and flour paste. Simmer until cooked and season to taste. ❧ Garnish with fried shallots and serve.

Opposite: (From top) Semur Ayam and Sop Ayam

Sate Ayam Madura
(Chicken Satay with Peanut Sauce)
~

400	grams chicken, cut into 1 x 2 cm pieces
2	tablespoons sweet soy sauce
1	tablespoon margarine, melted
	tomato, sliced
	shallots, sliced

Sambal Sate:

100	grams peanuts, roasted, skinned, fried, ground
2	red chillies, ground
5	bird's eye chillies, ground
50	cc sweet soy sauce
3	shallots, finely sliced
1	tablespoon lime juice

Thread 4–5 pieces chicken onto *sate* skewers. ↝ Mix sweet soy sauce and melted margarine. Dip each skewer in this sauce until the meat is completely covered. Grill until golden brown, turning skewers over from time to time. Serve with *sambal*, tomato and shallots.

Sambal Sate: Combine all the ingredients for *sambal*. Serve as a dip for *sate*.

Sate Ayam Banjar
(Chicken Satay with Black Shrimp Paste Sauce)
~

500	grams chicken meat, cut into 1 x 2 cm pieces
2	tablespoons sweet soy sauce
1	tablespoon margarine, melted

Black Shrimp Paste Sauce:

10	red chillies, boiled, ground
5	tablespoons tomato sauce
1	teaspoon black shrimp paste
5	cloves garlic, ground
2	tablespoons margarine, melted
	salt and sugar

Thread 4–5 pieces chicken onto satay skewers. ↝ Combine sweet soy sauce and margarine with 5 tablespoons of the black shrimp paste sauce. ↝ Dip each skewer into this sauce until the meat is completely covered. Let it stand for 30 minutes. ↝ Grill chicken over hot charcoal, turning skewers over from time to time. Serve with sweet soy sauce and the remaining black shrimp paste sauce.

Black Shrimp Paste Sauce: Combine all sauce ingredients. Serve as a dip.

Gulai Itik Hijau
(Duck in Green Chilli Sauce)
~

3	tablespoons oil
2	stalks lemon grass, bruised
5	kaffir lime leaves
1	young duck, cut into 8 pieces
750	cc water
2–3	pieces dried sour fruit (*Garcinia cambogia*)

Spices (ground):

200	grams green chillies
10	shallots
2	teaspoons chopped ginger
2	teaspoons chopped turmeric
2	tablespoons chopped galangal
1½	teaspoons peppercorns
8	candlenuts, roasted
	salt

Heat oil and sauté ground spices, lemon grass and kaffir lime leaves until fragrant, then add duck. ↝ Add enough water to cover the duck, then add dried sour fruit. Simmer for 2–3 hours until the duck is tender, the spices are absorbed and the gravy has thickened. Season to taste and serve.

Opposite: (From left) Sate Ayam Banjar and Sate Ayam Madura

Itik Masak Merah
(Duck in Red Chilli Sauce)

1 young duck, cut into 8 pieces
1 piece *asam gelugur*,
  soaked in 450 cc water
1 tablespoon salt
3 tablespoons oil
6 shallots, sliced
2 cloves garlic, sliced
1 stalk lemon grass, bruised
1–2 star anise
2 green cardamoms / 3 white cardamoms
1 litre coconut milk from 1 coconut
5 curry leaves

Spices (ground):
15 red chillies
1½ tablespoons coriander
1 teaspoon cumin, roasted
2 cloves, roasted
4 candlenuts, roasted
2 cm cinnamon stick
2 teaspoons *kas-kas* (white poppy seeds)
2 teaspoons chopped turmeric
2 teaspoons chopped ginger
5 shallots
2 cloves garlic
1 teaspoon salt

Rub duck with *asam gelugur* water and salt, and let it stand for 15 minutes. Then mix well with ground spices. ❖ Heat oil and sauté shallots and garlic until golden brown. Add spiced duck, lemon grass, star anise and cardamoms, and cook until juices from the duck have evaporated. Pour in the coconut milk and add curry leaves. ❖ Continue to cook until the duck is tender and the gravy has thickened.

Ayam Kalasan
(Fried Chicken with Chilli-Tomato Sauce)

1 chicken, cut into 4 pieces
100 cc coconut water
¼ teaspoon baking soda
5 cloves garlic, finely sliced
2 *salam* leaves (or bay leaves as a substitute)
1 cm galangal, bruised
  salt and brown sugar
  oil for deep-frying

Sambal:
150 grams red chillies, seeded
6 shallots
2 cloves garlic
1 red tomato, chopped
½ teaspoon dried shrimp paste
  salt and sugar

Simmer chicken with coconut water and other ingredients until the water has almost evaporated and the chicken is tender. Add water if necessary. Drain and allow to cool. ❖ Deep-fry chicken in hot oil until golden brown. Set aside. ❖ Brush chicken with the remaining sauce to give it a shine.

Sambal: Sauté red chillies, shallots, garlic, tomato and shrimp paste until half-cooked, then set aside. Grind and add salt and sugar. Add to the remaining chicken sauce. Sauté with 5 tablespoons oil over low heat.

Right: Ayam Kalasan
Opposite: (From left) Itik Masak Merah
and Gulai Itik Hijau (page 98)

MEAT

104 *Semur Betawi*
Fried Beef in Soy Sauce Gravy
—JAKARTA

Pallu Basa
Meat and Grated Coconut Curry
—SOUTH SULAWESI

106 *Pacah Daging*
Grilled Beef Marinated in Spicy Coconut
Milk—BENGKULU, SOUTH SUMATRA

Bistik Daging
Beef Steak

108 *Daging Asam*
Beef in Spiced and Tangy Gravy
—ACEH, NORTH SUMATRA

Dendeng Balado
Dried Spiced Beef—WEST SUMATRA

110 *Sandung Lamur Cabai Hijau*
Brisket with Green Chillies—JAVA

Sambal Goreng Kreni / Printil
Meat Balls in Coconut Milk—JAVA

112 *Sate Manis*
Sweet Satay—JAVA

Sate Padang
Padang Satay—WEST SUMATRA

114 *Galantin*
Meat and Glass Noodles Loaf—JAVA

Rawon
Brisket in Black Nut Sauce—EAST JAVA

116 *Gecok*
Beef Innards in Sesame Curry
—SUMBAWA, WEST LESSER SUNDA

Daging Empal
Sweet Fried Beef—JAVA

Dendeng Ragi
Beef with Shredded Coconut—JAVA

118 *Kalio Hati*
Beef Liver in Coconut Milk—SUMATRA

Gulai Banak / Otak
Beef Brain Curry—WEST SUMATRA

Rendang Daging
Beef in Spicy Coconut Milk
—WEST SUMATRA

120 *Bistik Lidah*
Ox Tongue Steak

Sop Buntut
Oxtail Soup

122 *Soto Madura*
Beef Innards and Glass Noodles Soup
—EAST JAVA

Soto Bandung
Beef and White Radish in Clear Soup
—WEST JAVA

124 *Soto Padang*
Spicy Beef Soup—WEST SUMATRA

Soto Betawi
Spiced Innards Soup—JAKARTA

126 *Gule Kambing*
Lamb Leg Curry—CENTRAL & EAST JAVA

Gulai Bagar
Lamb in Poppy Seed Curry
—NORTH SUMATRA

128 *Gulai Korma*
Lamb Curry—ACEH,
NORTH SUMATRA

Gulai Parsanga
Lamb Leg in Roasted Grated Coconut
Curry—MADURA, EAST JAVA

Kari Kambing
Lamb in Milk Curry—SUMATRA

130 *Krengsengan*
Spiced Lamb Fillet—East Java

Karang Binaci
Spicy Sweet-Sour Lamb Ribs
—MADURA, EAST JAVA

Rabeg
Lamb Innards in Spiced Soy Sauce
—WEST SUMATRA

132 *Mahbub*
Grilled Minced Lamb—WEST SUMATRA

Masam Padiah
Lamb and Bamboo Shoot Curry
—WEST SUMATRA

Kagape Kambing
Lamb in Thick Fried Coconut Sauce
—SUMBAWA, WEST LESSER SUNDA

134 *Tongseng*
Stir-fried Lamb in Sweet Soy Sauce
—CENTRAL JAVA

Sate Kambing
Lamb Satay—JAVA

136 *Perut Cuka*
Lamb Stomach in Sweet-Sour Sauce
—EAST LESSER SUNDA

Sop Kambing
Lamb Soup—WEST JAVA

Semur Betawi
(Fried Beef in Soy Sauce Gravy)
~

500	grams beef, thinly sliced
5	tablespoons sweet soy sauce
1	tablespoon margarine
5	shallots, finely sliced
1	*salam* leaf (or bay leaf as a substitute)
1/4	nutmeg, bruised
2	cloves
3	cm cinnamon stick
1/2	piece mace
1	tomato, chopped
1	tablespoon fried shallots
	salt

Spices (ground):

4	cloves garlic
1	teaspoon chopped ginger
3	candlenuts
2	teaspoons coriander
1/4	teaspoon cumin
1 1/2	teaspoons peppercorns

Combine beef with sweet soy sauce and mix thoroughly. Set aside. ❧ Heat margarine and gently fry shallots until golden brown. Add ground spices, *salam* leaf, nutmeg, cloves, cinnamon and mace. Fry until fragrant, then add beef with sweet soy sauce. When the ingredients are cooked, add water to cover beef. ❧ Cook until meat is tender and the gravy has thickened, then add chopped tomato. Serve hot with a sprinkle of fried shallots.

Optional: An additional 300 grams potatoes, quartered and fried until golden brown may be added after beef is tender. Beef can be replaced with fried bean curd or chicken.

Pallu Basa
(Meat and Grated Coconut Curry)
~

3	tablespoons oil
2	stalks lemon grass, bruised
1/2	nutmeg
3	cloves
5	cm cinnamon stick
1	kg beef, cut into pieces 1 x 3 x 5 cm
150	grams shredded coconut, roasted, ground
1	litre coconut milk from 1 coconut
2	tablespoons tamarind juice

Spices (ground):

2	tablespoons coriander
1/2	tablespoon peppercorns
1	teaspoon cumin
1/4	teaspoon aniseed
100	grams red chilli peppers
8	shallots
1 1/2	teaspoons chopped ginger
1	tablespoon chopped galangal
1	teaspoon salt

Heat oil and sauté ground spices, lemon grass, nutmeg, cloves and cinnamon until fragrant. Add beef and stir. Then add roasted coconut and coconut milk. Simmer and stir from time to time until the beef is tender and the gravy has thickened. Add the tamarind juice and simmer over low heat for 5 more minutes.

Opposite: (Clockwise from top) Pallu Basa, Pacah Daging, on skewers and served with sambal (page 106), and Semur Betawi

Pacah Daging
(Grilled Beef Marinated in Spicy Coconut Milk)

500   grams beef loin, cut into 2–3 pieces
150   cc thick coconut milk
       skewers

Spices (ground):
1   tablespoon coriander, roasted
1   teaspoon tamarind
1   teaspoon chopped turmeric
7   shallots
3   cloves garlic
    salt and brown sugar

Combine ground spices with coconut milk and beef. Stir until they are mixed thoroughly. Let the mixture stand for 1–2 hours. Remove beef from marinade and set aside. ❧ Thread the beef onto skewers and brush with the remaining marinade. Grill over hot charcoal until thoroughly cooked. ❧ Remove beef from the skewers and cut into bite-sized pieces. Serve with *sambal*.

Sambal: Combine 3 red chillies, sliced, with 3 finely sliced shallots (or with 1/2 onion, sliced) and 1 chopped tomato. Add 1 tablespoon lime juice and mix well.

Bistik Daging
(Beef Steak)

500   grams beef, cut into pieces 3/4 cm wide
1/4   teaspoon pepper
    nutmeg and salt to taste
2–3   tablespoons margarine

Sauce:
100   cc stock
2   cloves
1/4   nutmeg, bruised
1   tablespoon tomato sauce
1–2   teaspoons sweet soy sauce

Serve with:
200   grams carrots, cut and boiled
200   grams young french beans, boiled
250   grams potatoes, sliced 1/2 cm thick, fried

Tenderise beef by laying the pieces on a flat surface and pounding with the back of a knife. Rub beef with pepper, nutmeg and salt. ❧ Heat margarine in a pan and fry beef until golden brown. Remove from the pan and set aside. ❧ Serve beef with carrots, french beans, potatoes and sauce.

Sauce: Pour stock into the pan with the margarine from frying beef. Add the other sauce ingredients and simmer over low heat.

Opposite: Bistik Daging

Daging Asam
(Beef in Spiced and Tangy Gravy)
~

1	kg beef, cut into 2 cm cubes
2	tablespoons margarine
5	cloves garlic, sliced
10	shallots, finely sliced
1/2	nutmeg
3	cm cinnamon stick
3	cloves
3	cardamoms
1	litre coconut milk from 1 1/2 coconuts
250	grams potatoes, peeled, cut into 2 cm cubes
1–2	tablespoons tamarind juice
5	carambolas, cut into small pieces

Spices (ground):

1	tablespoon coriander
1/2	teaspoon cumin
1/2	teaspoon aniseed
1/2	teaspoon pepper
	salt

Combine beef with ground spices and knead until thoroughly mixed. Let it stand for 30 minutes. ❧ Heat margarine and sauté garlic until golden brown, then add shallots. Fry until soft. Add beef, nutmeg, cinnamon, cloves and cardamoms. Stir until fragrant, then pour in coconut milk. ❧ When the beef is nearly tender, add potatoes, tamarind juice and carambolas. Simmer until the ingredients are cooked and the gravy has thickened.

Dendeng Balado
(Dried Spiced Beef)
~

500	grams beef, fat and sinew removed, thinly sliced
4	tablespoons lime juice
8	tablespoons oil
6	shallots, finely sliced
4	kaffir lime leaves
15	red chillies, coarsely ground, or halved
1	teaspoon salt

Knead beef with 1–2 tablespoons lime juice, and let it stand for 10 minutes. Spread in a baking pan and dry in the sun until nearly crisp, or bake in an oven with low heat until the juices are absorbed. ❧ Heat oil and fry beef until cooked. Drain and set aside. ❧ Sauté shallots until golden brown, then add kaffir lime leaves and chillies. When the chillies are cooked, add remaining lime juice and salt. Then toss in beef and stir well.

Opposite: (From left) Daging Asam and Dendeng Balado

Sandung Lamur Cabai Hijau
(Brisket with Green Chillies)

3	tablespoons oil
3	cloves garlic, thinly sliced
7	shallots, thinly sliced
200	grams green chillies, sliced
50	grams red chillies, sliced
2	*salam* leaves (or bay leaves as a substitute)
1	cm galangal, bruised
1/2	teaspoon chopped lesser galangal
2	teaspoons thinly sliced lesser ginger
1/2	stalk lemon grass, bruised
350	grams brisket, boiled, cut into 1 x 1 x 2 cm pieces
250	cc meat stock
5	tablespoons sweet soy sauce
5	young tomatoes, quartered
	salt and sugar

Heat oil and fry garlic until golden brown. Add shallots and green chillies. Sauté until soft, then add red chillies, *salam* leaves, galangal, lesser galangal, lesser ginger, lemon grass and brisket. ❧ Pour in the stock and add sweet soy sauce, tomatoes, salt and sugar. Simmer over low heat until cooked. Remove from heat and serve.

Sambal Goreng Kreni / Printil
(Meat Balls in Coconut Milk)

500	grams minced beef
1	egg, lightly beaten
	salt
3	tablespoons oil
7	shallots, thinly sliced
2	*salam* leaves (or bay leaves as a substitute)
1	cm galangal, bruised
5	red chillies, seeded, thinly sliced
1	tomato, chopped
500	cc coconut milk
	salt

Spices (ground):

5	red chillies, seeded
3	cloves garlic
	salt and sugar

Combine minced beef with egg and salt. Shape mixture into balls and put on a tray. Brush meat balls with oil and steam until cooked. ❧ Heat oil and fry shallots until golden brown. Then add ground spices, *salam* leaves, galangal, chillies and tomato. Fry until meat is soft, then pour in coconut milk. Simmer over low heat, stirring from time to time. ❧ Add meatballs to the gravy and simmer over low heat. Continue stirring until the gravy is thick and oily. Season to taste.

Note: This dish is usually served with Yellow Rice (page 26) or spiced rice.

Opposite: (From left) Sambal Goreng Kreni / Printil and Sandung Lamur Cabai Hijau

Sate Manis
(Sweet Satay)
~

500	grams beef loin, cut into pieces $1/2$ x $1^1/_2$ x 2 cm
2	tablespoons lime juice
3	tablespoons sweet soy sauce
1	tablespoon oil

Spices (ground):

1	tablespoon coriander, roasted
$1/4$	teaspoon cumin, roasted
1	teaspoon peppercorns
4	cloves garlic
3	red chillies

Mix and knead beef with ground spices, lime juice, sweet soy sauce and oil. Let the mixture stand at least 15 minutes. ❧ Thread 4–5 pieces beef onto a skewer, brush it with remaining marinade and grill until golden brown. Serve with sweet soy sauce or peanut sauce, or both.

Sweet Soy Sauce: Grind 10 bird's eye chillies with 2 shallots, and combine with 3 tablespoons sweet soy sauce.

Peanut Sauce: Grind 1 red chilli with 100 grams roasted or fried peanuts. Add 100 cc water and stir well.

Sate Padang
(Padang Satay)
~

200	grams brisket
800	grams innards (heart, tripe, intestines, liver, lung)
$2^1/_2$	litres water
4	kaffir lime leaves
1	stalk lemon grass, bruised
1	turmeric leaf
1	piece dried sour fruit (*Garcinia cambogia*) skewers
1–2	tablespoons oil
50	grams rice flour and 1 tablespoon cornstarch, for every 500 cc stock fried shallots, for garnishing

Spices (ground):

8	red chillies
2	teaspoons coriander, roasted
1	teaspoon peppercorns
$1/4$	teaspoon cumin, roasted
6	shallots
1	teaspoon chopped turmeric
1	teaspoon chopped ginger
$1/2$	tablespoon chopped galangal

Boil brisket and innards until half-cooked. Then add ground spices, kaffir lime leaves, lemon grass, turmeric leaf and dried sour fruit. Add hot water if necessary. Simmer until the meat is tender. Remove brisket and innards and cut into 1 x 2 x 3 cm pieces. ❧ Thread meat onto the skewers, making sure that every skewer has brisket and various innards. Brush with oil and grill over hot charcoal until dry. ❧ Thicken the remaining marinade with rice flour and cornstarch mixed with a little water. ❧ Serve satay with *ketupat* (compressed rice cakes) or *lontong* (rice dumplings). Pour hot sauce over the meat and sprinkle with fried shallots.

Opposite: (From top) Sate Manis and Sate Padang

Galantin

(Meat and Glass Noodles Loaf)
~

500	grams minced beef
50	grams glass noodles, cut into 10 cm lengths, soaked until tender, drained
2	slices bread, cut into 1 cm cubes, soaked in hot water, squeezed
2	eggs, lightly beaten
1	teaspoon sweet soy sauce
1/2	teaspoon pepper
1/4	teaspoon powdered nutmeg
1	teaspoon salt

Sauce:

1	tablespoon margarine
1	clove garlic, finely sliced
4	shallots, finely sliced
150	cc stock
2	tablespoons sweet soy sauce
1	tablespoon tomato sauce
1/2	teaspoon pepper
1/4	teaspoon powdered nutmeg
1/2	teaspoon salt
1	teaspoon cornstarch, mixed with a little water

Combine beef with other ingredients and mix well. ❧ Clean a milk can and cover with banana leaf / plastic up to 2 cm from the top. ❧ Fill the can with beef mixture and steam until cooked. Remove from the steamer and let it cool. When cooled, remove the beef from the mould and fry with margarine. Slice into pieces 1 cm thick. ❧ Serve with sauce, fried potatoes and boiled vegetables.

Sauce: Heat margarine and fry garlic and shallots until soft, then pour in the stock. Add the other ingredients, stirring in cornstarch last, to thicken the sauce.

Note: If you don't have a can, you can put the mixture in the centre of a banana leaf and roll it up firmly into a cylindrical shape. Secure both ends, then steam.

Rawon

(Brisket in Black Nut Sauce)
~

3	tablespoons oil
1	stalk lemon grass, bruised
3	kaffir lime leaves
500	grams brisket, cut into 2 cm cubes
1 1/2	litres water

Spices (ground):

2	red chillies
3	candlenuts, roasted / fried
1	teaspoon coriander, roasted
1	teaspoon chopped turmeric
1	tablespoon chopped galangal
1/2	teaspoon dried shrimp paste
4	cloves garlic
8	shallots
3–4	black nuts, blanch the flesh, soak until tender, drain
1	teaspoon tamarind

Heat oil and fry ground spices, lemon grass and kaffir lime leaves until fragrant, then add brisket. Sauté until the colour changes, then add water. Simmer over low heat until the brisket is tender and ground spices are absorbed. Serve immediately.

Note: This dish is usually served with shrimp paste sauce (sambal terasi), short bean sprouts, salted egg or Telur Pindang (page 186) and prawn crackers. You may add 1 chayote, cut into 1 1/2 cm cubes, and string beans or french beans, and use only 100 grams beef.

Right: (From left) Gecok (recipe 116) and Rawon
Opposite: Galantin

Gecok
(Beef Innards in Sesame Curry)
~

500	grams beef innards or brisket
125	grams shredded coconut, roasted, finely pounded
75	grams sesame seeds, roasted, finely pounded
750	cc coconut milk from ½ coconut
6–7	carambolas, thinly sliced
½	teaspoon pepper
	salt
4	candlenuts, roasted / fried, ground
6	shallots, finely sliced
2	cm galangal, bruised
4	kaffir lime leaves, finely sliced
1–2	tablespoons fried shallots
2–3	limes, extract juice

Wash and cut boiled brisket / innards. ✧ Boil with pounded roasted coconut, pounded sesame seeds, coconut milk, sliced carambola, pepper, salt, candlenuts, sliced shallots and galangal. Cook until the meat is tender and the sauce has thickened. ✧ Spoon lime juice over meat and garnish with a sprinkle of finely sliced kaffir lime leaves and fried shallots.

Daging Empal
(Sweet Fried Beef)
~

750	grams beef, fat and sinew removed
1	*salam* leaf (or bay leaf as a substitute)
	oil

Spices (ground):

1	tablespoon chopped galangal
7	cloves garlic
1	teaspoon tamarind
1	tablespoon coriander, roasted
½	teaspoon cumin, roasted
	salt and brown sugar

Boil beef with *salam* leaf until tender. Remove and set aside. ✧ Cut beef into pieces 1 x 6 x 8 cm. Tenderise meat by pounding with the back of a knife. Mix ground spices with remaining stock and stir well. Add beef, and let it soak for 15 minutes. ✧ Remove beef and fry in oil until golden brown.

Note: Since brown sugar is used, the dish tastes rather sweet.

Dendeng Ragi
(Beef with Shredded Coconut)
~

500	grams beef, fat and sinew removed
½	tablespoon coriander powder
2–3	tablespoons brown sugar
1	teaspoon tamarind
1	teaspoon salt
1	coconut, skin removed, shredded
2	*salam* / bay leaves
1	stalk lemon grass, bruised
75	grams brown sugar

Spices (ground):

1	tablespoon coriander, roasted
1	teaspoon tamarind
5	cloves garlic
5	shallots
1	tablespoon chopped galangal

Slice beef and tenderise by pounding with the back of a knife. Mix beef with coriander powder and sugar, and knead until thoroughly mixed. ✧ Simmer over low heat until the juices are absorbed and the beef is tender. Set aside. ✧ Boil all the ingredients except the beef and brown sugar in 250 cc water until the water is absorbed. When shredded coconut turns golden brown, add brown sugar and beef. Stir until beef is completely covered with coconut.

Opposite: (From left) Dendeng Ragi and Daging Empal

Kalio Hati

(Beef Liver in Coconut Milk)

~

500	cc coconut milk from 1 coconut
1	turmeric leaf, torn, knotted
1	stalk lemon grass, bruised
3	kaffir lime leaves
1–2	pieces asam gelugur
500	grams beef liver, cut into 3 cm cubes

Spices (ground):

150	grams red chillies
1	tablespoon chopped galangal
1	teaspoon chopped ginger
1 1/2	teaspoons chopped turmeric
8	shallots
2	teaspoons coriander, roasted
	salt

Bring to the boil coconut milk with ground spices and other ingredients except liver. Cook until the gravy thickens. ❧ Add liver and simmer over low heat until the gravy is thick and oily. Remove the leaves before serving.

Optional: Beef can be substituted with chicken, egg or spleen.

Gulai Banak / Otak

(Beef Brain Curry)

~

1	beef brain, cleaned and steamed for 15 minutes until firm
750	cc coconut milk from 1 coconut
1/2	turmeric leaf
3	kaffir lime leaves
1	stalk lemon grass, bruised
3	cup leaves, finely sliced
20	basil leaves
1–2	pieces asam gelugur

Spices (ground):

10	red chillies
1	tablespoon chopped galangal
1	teaspoon chopped turmeric
2	teaspoons chopped ginger
8	shallots
1	teaspoon coriander, roasted

Cut steamed beef brain into serving pieces. ❧ Boil the coconut milk with ground spices and other ingredients. Stir from time to time. Continue to simmer over low heat, then add beef brain. Simmer until the beef brain is cooked and the gravy becomes oily.

Rendang Daging

(Beef in Spicy Coconut Milk)

~

1 1/4	litres coconut milk from 2 old coconuts
1	turmeric leaf, torn and knotted
5	kaffir lime leaves
1	stalk lemon grass, bruised
1–2	pieces asam gelugur
10	red chillies, finely sliced
1	kg beef, fat and sinew removed, cut into 3 cm cubes

Spices (ground):

3	tablespoons chopped galangal
1/2	tablespoon chopped turmeric
1/2	tablespoon chopped ginger
200	grams red chillies
4	shallots
	salt

Simmer coconut milk with turmeric leaf, kaffir lime leaves, lemon grass, asam gelugur, sliced chillies and ground spices until the milk thickens and becomes oily. Reduce heat. ❧ Add beef and cook until tender. Stir occasionally until the spices dry and turn brown.

Optional: Combine rendang with 300 grams small potatoes. ❧ Soak potatoes in water for 15 minutes then scrub with a soft brush to clean potato skin. Add to the gravy together with beef. ❧ Rendang can also be combined with 150 grams dried red peanuts (kacang jogo) which have been soaked for half an hour. Add together with beef.

Note: Rendang can be kept for a long time in the refrigerator. Heat before serving.

Opposite: (Clockwise from top) Kalio Hati, Gulai Banak / Otak and Rendang Daging

Bistik Lidah
(Ox Tongue Steak)

1	fresh ox tongue
2	*salam* leaves (or bay leaves as a substitute)
1	teaspoon peppercorns
3	shallots, coarsely chopped

Sour Sauce:

75	grams margarine
25	grams flour
500	cc stock
1/4	teaspoon pepper
1	teaspoon salt
	sugar
2–3	tablespoons lime juice

Serve with:

200	grams white beans, boiled until tender, or canned white beans, drained
250	grams fresh mushrooms, boiled, or canned mushrooms, drained
200	grams french beans, boiled, cut into 3 cm pieces
	mashed potatoes

Boil fresh tongue with *salam* / bay leaves, peppercorns and chopped shallots until half-cooked. Remove tongue from the stock and peel off the skin. ❧ Put boiled tongue back into the stock and simmer until tender. Remove from the pan, slice thinly, and arrange on a serving plate. ❧ Serve with white beans, mushrooms, french beans, mashed potatoes and sour sauce.

Sour Sauce: Heat 25 grams margarine. Add flour and stir well. Pour in the meat stock gradually, stirring continuously until the mixture is smooth. Add a dash of salt, pepper and sugar. Simmer over low heat, then add lime juice and stir well. Remove from heat, add remaining margarine and mix well.

Mashed Potatoes: Mash 500 grams boiled potatoes, then add 100 cc milk, 1 tablespoon margarine, pepper and ground nutmeg. Cook over low heat, stirring from time to time until the mixture is dry.

Sop Buntut
(Oxtail Soup)

1	kg oxtail / beef tail, cut into serving pieces
1/2	tablespoon chopped ginger
1/2	nutmeg, bruised
1	spring onion, cut into 2–3 pieces
1	tablespoon margarine
200	grams carrots, cut into 3 cm pieces, then halved or quartered
250	grams potatoes, cut into 4–6 pieces
	salt

Spices (ground):

6	shallots
3	cloves garlic
1	teaspoon peppercorns

Garnishing:

fried shallots, spring onions, chopped Chinese parsley and melinjo nut crackers

Put oxtail in a pan with 2 litres water and bring to the boil. Carefully scoop off and discard the scum floating on the surface. Discard the stock and replace with 2 litres clean water. ❧ Add chopped ginger, nutmeg and spring onion. Cover the pan and simmer over low heat until tender. Remove the tail, reserving 1 1/2 litres stock. Bring the stock to the boil, then add oxtail. ❧ Heat margarine and fry ground spices until fragrant. Add to the boiling stock, then add carrots and potatoes. Bring to the boil until the ingredients are thoroughly cooked. ❧ Garnish with fried shallots, spring onions, Chinese parsley and melinjo nut crackers. Serve hot.

Opposite: (From top) Sop Buntut and Bistik Lidah

Soto Madura
(Beef Innards and Glass Noodles Soup)

750	grams innards (heart, tripe, intestines, brain, liver, lung, spleen)
250	grams brisket, cut into serving pieces
2	stalks lemon grass, bruised
5	kaffir lime leaves
	salt

Spices (ground):

2	teaspoons peppercorns
2	tablespoons chopped ginger
1	teaspoon chopped turmeric
10	shallots
5	cloves garlic

Serve with:

50	grams glass noodles, cut into 10 cm lengths, soaked until tender, drained
2–3	tablespoons fried shallots
	Chinese parsley, finely chopped
	spring onion, finely sliced
	sweet soy sauce
	lime, sliced

Spicy Sauce (ground):

5	bird's eye chillies, steamed
3	shallots, steamed
5	candlenuts, roasted / fried
	salt

Clean tripe with boiling water or with lime (*kapur sirih*). Boil intestines until tender, then discard the water. Clean beef brain then steam until cooked. ❧ Boil brisket, tripe, heart, lung, spleen and liver until tender. Remove from the water and reserve 1 1/2 litres of stock. Slice innards thinly. ❧ Heat oil and fry ground spices until fragrant, then add lemon grass and kaffir lime leaves. Cook until soft, then add to the stock. Simmer over low heat until cooked.

How to serve: Put a portion of glass noodles in a bowl and arrange a few pieces of brisket and innards on top. Sprinkle with fried shallots, Chinese parsley, spring onion and sweet soy sauce. Add a slice or two or lime and serve with spicy sauce.

Note: To thicken the stock, add 2 teaspoons ground rice mixed with water.

Soto Bandung
(Beef and White Radish in Clear Soup)

350	grams brisket or offal
2	litres water
2	*salam* leaves (or bay leaves as a substitute)
1	cm galangal, bruised
1/2	teaspoon salt
1/2	teaspoon pepper
1	clove garlic, finely sliced, fried
75	grams white soybeans, blanched, cooled
200	grams white radish, peeled and sliced
2	spring onions, finely sliced
2	sprigs Chinese parsley, finely sliced
2	tablespoons fried shallots

Spicy Sauce:

15	bird's eye chillies, boiled, ground
1	tablespoon water
1/2	teaspoon vinegar
	salt

Serve with:

	sweet soy sauce
	lime, sliced

Combine all the ingredients for spicy sauce and mix well. ❧ Boil beef with *salam* leaves, galangal and salt until tender. Remove beef from the pot, reserving 1 1/2 litres stock. Cut beef into 1 cm cubes, and add to the stock. Add pepper and fried garlic. Bring to the boil. Add radish to beef stock and simmer until cooked. ❧ Drain soybeans and add a dash of salt. Fry until golden brown and dry, then drain. ❧ Serve soup garnished with spring onion, Chinese parsley, fried soybeans and fried shallots. ❧ Serve with spicy sauce, sweet soy sauce and slices of lime.

Opposite: (From left) Soto Madura and Soto Bandung

Soto Padang
(Spicy Beef Soup)

500	grams beef, fat and sinew removed
2	litres water
3	tablespoons oil
5	kaffir lime leaves
1	stalk lemon grass, bruised
1/2	nutmeg, bruised
2	cloves
2	spring onions, finely sliced
1/2	tablespoon vinegar
50	grams glass noodles, cut into 10 cm lengths, soaked until tender, drained
	potato croquettes (from page 76)
	fried shallots
	prawn crackers
	spring onions, sliced
	Chinese parsley, chopped
	sweet soy sauce

Spices (ground):

6	shallots
3	cloves garlic
1	teaspoon chopped ginger
1/2	teaspoon chopped turmeric
1	teaspoon peppercorns
	salt

Spicy Sauce (ground):

5	bird's eye chillies, steamed
3	red onions, steamed
	salt

Boil beef until tender. Remove from the stock and slice thinly. Tenderise meat by pounding with the back of a knife. Rub with a little salt and deep-fry until dry. Shred the meat finely. ❧ Simmer 1 1/4 litres stock; if there is not enough stock, add more water. ❧ Heat oil and gently fry ground spices, kaffir lime leaves, lemon grass, nutmeg and cloves until fragrant. Add these to the stock. Then add sliced spring onions and vinegar.

How to serve: Arrange glass noodles, sliced potatoes croquettes and fried beef in a bowl. Pour the hot stock over, and garnish with fried shallots, prawn crackers, spring onions and Chinese parsley. ❧ Serve with spicy sauce and sweet soy sauce.

Soto Betawi
(Spiced Innards Soup)

5	tablespoons oil
3	salam leaves (or bay leaves as a substitute)
5	cm cinnamon stick
1/2	nutmeg, bruised
250	grams brisket, boiled, cut into 1 x 2 cm pieces
1	kg innards (heart, tripe, intestines, liver, lung), boiled, cut into 1 x 2 cm pieces
1	litre stock
500	cc thick coconut milk from 1 coconut
2	sprigs Chinese parsley, finely chopped
3	spring onions, finely sliced
3	tomatoes, cut into wedges
3	tablespoons fried shallots
1	lime, sliced
3–4	tablespoons sweet soy sauce
100	grams melinjo nut crackers

Spices (ground):

6	cloves garlic
10	shallots
2	teaspoons chopped ginger
2	teaspoons chopped galangal
1/2	tablespoon coriander
2	teaspoons peppercorns
1/2	teaspoon cumin, roasted
3	candlenuts, roasted

Sauté ground spices, salam / bay leaves, cinnamon and nutmeg until fragrant. Then add the brisket and innards, and stir well. Pour in the stock and simmer over low heat until cooked. Add coconut milk, and continue to stir from time to time. Simmer over low heat until fragrant.

How to serve: Arrange sliced beef and innards in a serving bowl, then add Chinese parsley, spring onions and tomatoes. Garnish with a sprinkle of fried shallots and pour the hot gravy over. ❧ Serve with sliced lime, sweet soy sauce, melinjo nut crackers and spicy sauce.

Opposite: (From left) Soto Padang and Soto Betawi

Gule Kambing
(Lamb Leg Curry)

3	tablespoons oil
3	cloves
5	cm cinnamon stick
2	cardamoms
4	fenugreek seeds
1	stalk lemon grass, bruised
3	kaffir lime leaves
1	kg leg of lamb, chopped into serving pieces
750	cc thin coconut milk
250	cc thick coconut milk
1	tablespoon tamarind juice
	salt
	fried shallots, for garnishing

Spices (ground):

4	red chillies
3	cloves garlic
6	shallots
4	candlenuts, roasted
2	teaspoons coriander, roasted
1	teaspoon peppercorns
1/4	teaspoon cumin, roasted
10	aniseeds, roasted
1	teaspoon chopped ginger
1	teaspoon chopped turmeric
1/2	tablespoon chopped galangal

Heat oil and gently fry ground spices until fragrant, then add other spices, lemon grass and kaffir lime leaves. Stir until soft. Add meat and continue to cook until the colour changes. Add thin coconut milk and simmer until the meat is half-cooked. ❧ Pour in thick coconut milk and simmer until meat is tender. Add tamarind juice, season with salt and bring to the boil. ❧ Serve with a sprinkle of fried shallots.

Gulai Bagar
(Lamb in Poppy Seed Curry)

1–2	teaspoons oil / butter
10	shallots, finely sliced
4	cloves garlic, finely sliced
1	stalk lemon grass, bruised
1	kg lamb, chopped into large pieces
500	cc thin coconut milk
1–2	pieces dried sour fruit (*Garcinia cambogia*)
250	cc thick coconut milk
	salt

Spices (roasted and ground):

1	tablespoon coriander
1/2	teaspoon cumin
1/4	teaspoon aniseed
3	cm cinnamon stick
3	cloves
1/4	nutmeg
1	teaspoon peppercorns
2	tablespoons *kas-kas* (white poppy seeds)

Spices (ground):

8–10	fresh red chillies
2	teaspoons chopped ginger
1	teaspoon chopped turmeric
1/2	tablespoon chopped galangal

Heat oil / butter and gently fry shallots and garlic until golden brown. Add lemon grass and ground spices and fry until fragrant. Add meat and stir for a few minutes. ❧ Pour in thin coconut milk and add dried sour fruit. Cook until the gravy boils and the meat is half-cooked. ❧ Pour in thick coconut milk, stirring continuously until the meat is tender and the gravy is thick and greasy. Season with salt to taste.

Opposite: (Clockwise from top) Gulai Korma (page 128),
Gule Kambing and Gulai Bagar

Gulai Korma

(Lamb Curry)
~

2–3	tablespoons margarine
5	cloves garlic, finely sliced
10	shallots, finely sliced
5	cm cinnamon stick
2	cardamoms
1/2	nutmeg, bruised
1	stalk lemon grass, bruised
3	kaffir lime leaves
1–2	pieces dried sour fruit (*Garcinia cambogia*)
1	kg lamb, cut into 3 x 3 cm pieces
750 cc	thin coconut milk
250 cc	thick coconut milk
300	grams potatoes, halved or quartered
	salt

Spices (roasted and ground):
1	tablespoon coriander
1/2	teaspoon cumin
1/4	teaspoon aniseed
1/2	tablespoon peppercorns
3	cloves

Heat margarine and sauté garlic and shallots until golden brown. Add ground spices, other spices and herbs and meat. Continue to fry for a few minutes, then add thin coconut milk. ~ Simmer until the meat is half-cooked. Add thick coconut milk, potatoes and salt. ~ Cook and stir from time to time until the ingredients are cooked and the gravy has thickened.

Gulai Parsanga

(Lamb Leg in Roasted Grated Coconut Curry)
~

1	kg leg of lamb, chopped into serving pieces
1	tablespoon powdered coriander
1/2	teaspoon powdered cumin
1/4	teaspoon powdered aniseed
3	tablespoons oil
8	shallots, sliced
2	cardamoms, bruised
2	cloves
1/2	nutmeg, bruised
5	cm cinnamon stick
1	stalk lemon grass, bruised

1	litre coconut milk from 1/2 coconut
200	grams shredded coconut, roasted until golden brown, ground

Spices (ground):
3	cloves garlic
1	teaspoon chopped ginger
1	teaspoon chopped turmeric
1/2	tablespoon chopped galangal
	salt

Combine and knead lamb meat with powered coriander, cumin and aniseed. Let it stand for 10 minutes. ~ Heat oil and gently fry shallots until golden brown. Add ground spices, cardamoms, cloves, nutmeg, cinnamon and lemon grass. Continue to stir until fragrant. Add meat and stir from time to time. ~ Add coconut milk and ground coconut. Cook until the meat is tender and the gravy has thickened. Serve hot.

Kari Kambing

(Lamb in Milk Curry)
~

2	tablespoons oil
4	cloves garlic, finely sliced
5	shallots, finely sliced
3	cm cinnamon stick
1	star anise
3	cardamoms
3	cloves
500	grams lamb, sliced into pieces 3 x 4 x 5 cm
1	litre water
50	cc evaporated milk / 150 cc diluted milk
1	tomato, chopped
	salt

Spices (ground):
2	tablespoons coriander
1/2	teaspoon cumin, roasted
1/2–1	teaspoon aniseed
10	dried chillies / 15 fresh chillies
1	teaspoon chopped ginger
1/2	teaspoon chopped turmeric
2	cloves garlic
5	shallots

Heat oil and sauté garlic until golden brown. Add shallots, stir until soft, then add ground and whole spices. Continue to stir until fragrant. ~ Add meat, water, milk, tomato and salt. Cook until the gravy thickens.

Krengsengan
(Spiced Lamb Fillets)
~

3	tablespoons oil
1–2	tomatoes, chopped
350	grams lamb fillet, chopped into pieces 1 x 2 x 3 cm
200	cc water
1	tablespoon sweet soy sauce
1	tablespoon black shrimp paste
2	red chillies, seeded, finely sliced

Spices (ground):

5	shallots
2	cloves garlic
1/2	teaspoon peppercorns
1	teaspoon chopped ginger
	salt and sugar

Heat oil and gently fry the ground spices until golden brown. Add tomatoes and meat, and stir until the colour changes. ❧ Add water, sweet soy sauce and black shrimp paste. Cook until the meat is tender and the sauce is reduced. Add sliced chillies, stirring frequently until cooked. Serve hot.

Karang Binaci
(Spicy Sweet-Sour Lamb Ribs)
~

1	kg lamb ribs, chopped into serving pieces
3	tablespoons oil
1	litre water
3–4	tablespoons sweet soy sauce
1–2	teaspoons vinegar
	salt

Spices (ground):

5	red chillies
1	teaspoon peppercorns
1 1/2	teaspoons chopped ginger
8	shallots
4	cloves garlic

Knead meat with ground spices to mix thoroughly, and let it for stand for 10 minutes. ❧ Heat oil and fry the meat until it changes colour. Add water, sweet soy sauce, vinegar and salt. ❧ Cook until the sauce has completely dried up.

Rabeg
(Lamb Innards in Spiced Soy Sauce)
~

300	grams young lamb intestines, braided and boiled
300	grams tripe of young lamb, cover with boiling water, peel off black layer
300	grams lung, spleen and heart of lamb
5	tablespoons oil
3	cloves garlic, finely sliced
5	shallots, sliced
5	red chillies, finely sliced
2	teaspoons sliced ginger
2	*salam* leaves (or bay leaves as a substitute)
1	piece galangal, bruised
250	cc water
5	tablespoons sweet soy sauce
1–2	tablespoons tamarind juice
1/2	teaspoon pepper
	salt and sugar

Chop innards into 3 cm pieces. Gently fry the pieces until rather crisp. Remove, drain and set aside. ❧ Heat oil and sauté garlic and shallots until golden brown. Add red chillies, ginger, *salam* leaves and galangal. Continue to stir until spices become rather dry. Add innards, water, sweet soy sauce, tamarind juice, pepper, salt and sugar. ❧ Cook until the sauce is reduced. Remove from heat and serve.

Preceding page: (Clockwise from right) Krengsengan, Kari Kambing (page 128) and Gulai Parsanga (page 128)

Opposite: (From left) Rabeg and Karang Binaci

Mahbub
(Grilled Minced Lamb)
~

300	grams lamb, minced
200	grams lamb liver, minced
200	grams lamb fat fresh / dried, cut into 6 x 6 cm pieces
	skewers, banana leaves

Spices (ground):

1	tablespoon coriander
1/4	teaspoon cumin, roasted
1	teaspoon peppercorns
1/4	teaspoon powdered nutmeg
1/4	teaspoon powdered cloves
2	tablespoons fried shallots
1	tablespoon tamarind juice
	salt and sugar

Combine meat and liver with ground spices. Knead to mix thoroughly. Divide mixture into 16–17 parts. ❧ Shape meat into balls and wrap with fat. Thread meatballs onto skewers and wrap with banana leaves. ❧ Grill over hot charcoal until tender. Unwrap before serving.

Masam Padiah
(Lamb and Bamboo Shoot Curry)
~

1	kg lamb without fat, thinly sliced
5	tablespoons oil
1	stalk lemon grass, bruised
3	kaffir lime leaves
1	litre water
3–4	tablespoons tamarind juice
150	grams bamboo shoots, boiled, finely sliced
4	green chillies, halved
	salt

Spices (ground):

10	red chillies
5	candlenuts, roasted / fried
2	teaspoons powdered coriander
1	teaspoon chopped ginger
1	teaspoon chopped turmeric
2	teaspoons chopped galangal
7	shallots
3	cloves garlic

Gently fry lamb until golden brown, then set aside. ❧ Sauté ground spices, lemon grass and kaffir lime leaves until fragrant, then add meat, water and tamarind juice. Bring to the boil. ❧ Add bamboo shoots and green chillies and cook until the meat is tender and the sauce has reduced. Season with salt.

Note: To sweeten the dish, add 1 teaspoon sugar.

Kagape Kambing
(Lamb in Thick Fried Coconut Sauce)
~

500	grams lamb, cut into 2 x 2 x 3 cm pieces
1/2	teaspoon tamarind
1/2	teaspoon salt
3	tablespoons oil
1	stalk lemon grass, bruised
500	cc coconut milk from 1/2 coconut
1/2	coconut (200 grams), shredded, roasted, pounded

Spices (ground):

1	tablespoon coriander
2	teaspoons peppercorns, roasted
1/2	teaspoon cumin
2	candlenuts
2	teaspoons turmeric
2	teaspoons chopped ginger
2	teaspoons chopped galangal
4	cloves garlic
7	shallots
	salt

Combine and knead meat with tamarind and salt. Let it stand for 15 minutes. ❧ Heat oil and sauté ground spices and lemon grass until fragrant. Add meat and pour in coconut milk. Simmer until the meat is half-cooked, then add pounded coconut. Cook until the meat is tender and the gravy has thickened.

Opposite: (Clockwise from top) Masam Padiah, Mahbub and Kagape Kambing

Tongseng
(Stir-fried Lamb in Sweet Soy Sauce)
~

3	tablespoons oil
2	cloves garlic, finely chopped
5	shallots, finely chopped
3	red chillies, finely sliced
350	grams lamb, cut into 2 cm cubes
500	cc water
3–4	tablespoons sweet soy sauce
$^1/_2$	teaspoon pepper
	salt and sugar
5	cabbage leaves, cut into 2 x 2 cm pieces
1–2	tablespoons lime juice

Heat oil and gently fry garlic until golden brown, then add shallots and chillies. Continue frying until ingredients become soft. ❧ Add meat and stir frequently. Add water, sweet soy sauce, pepper, salt and sugar. Simmer until the meat is tender and the gravy has thickened. Add cabbage and lime juice. Cook until tender.

Sate Kambing
(Lamb Satay)
~

300	grams young lamb meat, cut into pieces 1$^1/_2$ x 2 x 3 cm
150	grams lamb liver, cut into pieces 1$^1/_2$ x 2 x 3 cm
1	tablespoon sweet soy sauce
$^1/_2$	tablespoon oil / melted margarine

Sambal (Spicy) Sweet Soy Sauce:

2	red chillies, boiled, finely sliced
5	bird's eye chillies, boiled, finely sliced
25	cc water
4–5	tablespoons sweet soy sauce
1–2	tomatoes, chopped into small pieces, or lime juice
2	shallots, finely sliced
4	kaffir lime leaves, finely sliced

Thread 4–5 pieces of meat and liver onto skewer. Combine sweet soy sauce with oil, and dip meat into this mixture. Grill over hot charcoal until golden brown. Serve immediately with *sambal* sweet soy sauce or peanut sauce.

Sambal Sweet Soy Sauce: Combine chillies with water and stir well. Add sweet soy sauce, tomatoes, shallots and lime leaves.

Peanut Sauce: Fry 2 tablespoons peanuts, then pound until fine. Combine with 2–3 tablespoons water, then add sweet soy sauce and sliced shallots.

Note: Lamb satay from East Java is usually eaten with sweet soy sauce. West Javanese like to eat satay with peanut sauce.

Opposite: (From left) Tongseng and Sate Kambing

Perut Cuka

(Lamb Stomach in Sweet-Sour Sauce)

1	kg lamb tripe / intestines
5	stalks lemon grass, bruised
5	tablespoons oil
35	cc water
1–2	tablespoons vinegar or
	3–4 tablespoons lime juice
	salt and sugar

Spices (ground):

50	grams bird's eye chillies
5	cloves garlic
10	shallots
2	teaspoons turmeric
1	teaspoon chopped ginger
1	tablespoon chopped galangal

Clean intestines and tripe, and bring to the boil with 2 stalks lemon grass until tender. Cut into 4 cm pieces. ❧ Heat oil and sauté ground spices and remaining lemon grass until fragrant. Add intestines and tripe and stir well. Add water, vinegar, salt and sugar. ❧ Simmer over low heat until the spices are absorbed and the sauce has thickened.

Sop Kambing

(Lamb Soup)

1	kg lamb, chopped into small pieces
2½	litres water
5	cm ginger, bruised
1	nutmeg, bruised
	salt
1	tablespoon margarine
3	spring onions, chopped into 2 cm pieces
250	grams carrots, cut into big pieces
½	teaspoon pepper
1–2	tomatoes, quartered
150	grams cabbage, cut into 3 cm pieces
2	sprigs Chinese parsley, chopped
4–5	limes, extract juice
2	tablespoons fried shallots
	melinjo nut crackers

Boil meat with ginger, nutmeg and salt until the meat is tender. Reserve 1½ litres stock. ❧ Heat margarine and sauté spring onions until soft, then add carrots. Pour in the stock and bring to the boil. Add pepper, tomato, cabbage and Chinese parsley. ❧ Simmer until cooked and season to taste. Sprinkle with lime juice and garnish with fried shallots and melinjo nut crackers.

Opposite: (From left) Perut Cuka and Sop Kambing

SEAFOOD

140 *Gulai Ikan*
Herbal Fish Curry—SUMATRA

Gulai Kepala Ikan
Fish Head Curry—ACEH,
NORTH SUMATRA

142 *Gulai Lemak Manis*
Fish in Sweet Curry—SUMATRA

Gulai Telur Ikan
Fish Roe Curry—SUMATRA

Ikan Air Garam
Fish Head in Clear Soup
—TERNATE, HALMAHERA

144 *Pindang Serani*
Fish in Turmeric Gravy—JAVA

Ikan Bumbu Bali
Balinese Spicy Fish—JAVA

146 *Pecak Lele*
Grilled Fish in Hot Sauce
—CENTRAL JAVA

Pepes Ikan Mas
Grilled Carp—WEST JAVA

148 *Sate Ikan*
Fish and Glass Noodles in Banana
Leaf—PALEMBANG, SOUTH SUMATRA

Pindang Kecap
Milkfish in Sweet Soy Sauce
—WEST JAVA

150 *Sepat Banang*
Milkfish with Mango and Prawns
—SUMBAWA, WEST LESSER SUNDA

Panggang Haruan
Grilled Catfish Stuffed with Chilli
—KALIMANTAN

152 *Sate Bandeng*
Grilled Stuffed Milkfish—BANTEN,
EAST JAVA

Ikan Mas Woku
Carp in Herbal Curry—NORTH SULAWESI

154 *Arsik*
Carp Stuffed with Herbs and Spices
—BATAK, NORTH SUMATRA

Udang Pedas
Spicy Prawns and Green Beans

156 *Sate Lilit*
Minced Fish Satay—BALI

Japit Udang
Prawn Satay—MADURA, EAST JAVA

Mangut Ikan Pe
Fish and Chayote in Coconut Milk
—JEPARA, CENTRAL JAVA

158 *Pelas Udang*
Spiced Shrimps Grilled in Banana
Leaf—MADURA, EAST JAVA

Tumis Udang
Stir-fried Prawns in Coconut Gravy
—ACEH, NORTH SUMATRA

Rajungan Goreng
Chilli Crabs—TAPANULI,
NORTH SUMATRA

160 *Kare Kepiting*
Crab Curry—EAST JAVA

Tumis Nus
Stir-fried Squid—BALI

162 *Sambal Kerang*
Cockles in Spiced Shredded Coconut
—SUMATRA

Sambal Tuk-tuk
Shredded Salted Fish with Green
Beans—TAPANULI, NORTH SUMATRA

Sambal Udang
Prawns in Chilli and Candlenut Gravy
—SIBOLGA, NORTH SUMATRA

164 *Palai Bada*
Whitebait and Herbs Grilled in Banana
Leaf—SIBOLGA, NORTH SUMATRA

Sop Tekwan
Fish Ball Soup—SOUTH SULAWESI

Gulai Ikan
(Herbal Fish Curry)
~

500	grams tuna / mackerel / snapper
1	litre coconut milk from 1 coconut
1	stalk lemon grass, bruised
2	pink ginger buds, cut into 2–4 pieces (if available)
3	cup leaves, coarsely sliced
1–2	slices *asam gelugur* or 1–2 tablespoons tamarind juice salt
25	grams basil leaves

Spices (ground):

75–100	grams red chillies
6	shallots
2	teaspoons chopped turmeric
2	teaspoons chopped ginger
1/2	tablespoon galangal

Clean fish and scrape the skin to remove scales. Rinse the fish under cold water, then cut off the fins and gills. Cut into 2–3 pieces depending on the size. Wash and drain. ⁖ Boil the coconut milk with ground spices, lemon grass, ginger buds, cup leaves, *asam gelugur* and salt. ⁖ Add fish and basil leaves. Allow to simmer until cooked. Stir frequently to prevent coconut milk from curdling.

Note: Fish can be replaced with shrimps or squid. If you are using squid, combine with spices and lemon grass and cook in a closed pan until the excess water has been absorbed. Add other ingredients and green beans.

Gulai Kepala Ikan
(Fish Head Curry)
~

1	fish head (850 grams), cut into 2–4 pieces lime juice and salt
2	tablespoons desiccated coconut, roasted, pounded
3	tablespoons oil
1	stalk lemon grass, bruised
1	pandanus leaf, torn, knotted
750	cc coconut milk from 1 coconut
5	carambolas, halved
10	*salam* leaves (or bay leaves as a substitute)

Spices (ground):

10	dried red chillies / 15 fresh chillies
1/2	tablespoon chopped turmeric
1/2	tablespoon chopped ginger
7	shallots
3	cloves garlic
1	tablespoon coriander, roasted
1/2	teaspoon cumin, roasted
1/4	teaspoon aniseed, roasted
1	teaspoon peppercorns, roasted
1	tablespoon dried carambola salt

Rub fish head with lime juice and salt, and let it stand for 1/2 hour. Drain, then rub the fish head with pounded coconut. ⁖ Heat oil and sauté ground spices, lemon grass and pandanus leaf until fragrant, then add coconut milk. Allow to simmer. Add fish head and carambolas, and bring to the boil. Stir from time to time, then add *salam* leaves. ⁖ Simmer until the fish is cooked and the gravy is a little oily.

Note: If there are no dried carambolas available, use 1/2 teaspoon tamarind juice.

Opposite: (Clockwise from top) Gulai Kepala Ikan, Gulai Ikan and Gulai Lemak Manis (page 142)

Gulai Lemak Manis
(Fish in Sweet Curry)

500 grams fish (snapper / Spanish mackerel / grouper / mackerel / yellow tail, etc.)
1 teaspoon chopped turmeric
1/2 teaspoon salt
 oil for deep-frying
3 tablespoons oil
6 shallots, thinly sliced
1 stalk lemon grass, bruised
4 red chillies, sliced
500 cc coconut milk
1 piece *asam gelugur*
 salt
2 pink ginger buds, halved
4 carambolas, halved

Spices (ground):
2 teaspoons turmeric
2 teaspoons chopped ginger
1 tablespoon chopped galangal

Cut fish and rub with chopped turmeric and 1/2 teaspoon salt. Let it stand for 10 minutes. Deep-fry until the fish turns golden brown, then set aside. ❧ Heat 3 tablespoons oil and sauté shallots then add ground spices, lemon grass and chillies. Pour in coconut milk and add *asam gelugur*, salt and ginger buds. Bring to the boil. ❧ Add fish and carambolas. Cook until the gravy thickens.

Gulai Telur Ikan
(Fish Roe Curry)

500 grams fish roe
1–2 tablespoons lime juice
 salt
5 tablespoons oil
1 stalk lemon grass, bruised
5 curry leaves
1/2 pandanus leaf, torn, knotted
500 cc coconut milk from 1/2 coconut
2 green chillies, halved
2 red chillies, halved

Spices (ground):
7 dried chillies / 10 fresh chillies
2 teaspoons coriander
1/4 teaspoon aniseed, roasted
1/2 teaspoon cumin
1 tablespoon shredded coconut
1/2 tablespoon dried carambola
1 1/2 teaspoons chopped ginger
1 teaspoon chopped turmeric
2 cloves garlic
5 shallots
 salt

Rub fish roe with lime juice and salt, and let it stand for 10 minutes. Combine ground spices with the fish roe. Heat oil and sauté the roe until it hardens, then add lemon grass and curry and pandanus leaves. When fragrant, pour in coconut milk and add chillies. ❧ Simmer over low heat until cooked.

Ikan Air Garam
(Fish Head in Clear Soup)

1 (850 grams) snapper / grouper head
1 teaspoon vinegar
1 litre water
2 cm galangal, bruised
3 stalks lemon grass, bruised
4 cm ginger, bruised
1/2 tablespoon salt
200 grams tomatoes, each cut into 4–6 pieces
3 spring onions, cut into 3 cm lengths
8 unpeeled shallots, roasted, peeled and thinly sliced
4 red chillies, sliced
25 grams basil leaves
1 lime, extract juice

Rub fish head with 1 teaspoon vinegar and let it stand for 30 minutes. Wash and drain. ❧ Bring to the boil water with galangal, lemon grass and ginger, then add salt. After a few minutes, add fish head, tomatoes, spring onions and shallots. Allow to simmer. ❧ When the ingredients are almost cooked, add sliced chillies and basil leaves. Simmer over low heat. Before removing from heat, season and add lime juice to taste.

Note: You can add sugar if you like. If no fish head is available, use a whole fish.

Opposite: (From left) Ikan Air Garam and Gulai Telur Ikan

Pindang Serani
(Fish in Turmeric Gravy)
~

500	grams gray mullet / milkfish
1–2	tablespoons lime juice
	salt and sugar
750	cc water
2	stalks lemon grass, bruised
1	cm galangal, bruised
3	cm ginger, thinly sliced lengthwise
6	cm turmeric, thinly sliced lengthwise
8	shallots, thinly sliced
3	cloves garlic, thinly sliced
2	tomatoes, quartered or 10 carambolas, halved

Rub fish with lime juice and salt, and let it stand for 15 minutes. Wash and drain. ❧ Bring water to the boil and add all ingredients except fish. Simmer over low heat. ❧ When the gravy turns yellow, add fish. Reduce heat and continue cooking. ❧ Simmer until the fish is cooked and the spices are absorbed. Season to taste.

Ikan Bumbu Bali
(Balinese Spicy Fish)
~

500	grams pomfret / Spanish mackerel / snapper / milkfish, cut into 3–4 pieces
1	lime, extract juice
1	teaspoon salt
	oil
2	stalks lemon grass, bruised
1	teaspoon tamarind juice
1	tablespoon sweet soy sauce

Spices (ground):

5	red chillies, seeded
5	shallots
2	cloves garlic
3	candlenuts
1	teaspoon chopped ginger
1	teaspoon salt

Rub fish with lime juice and salt, and let it stand for 15 minutes. Wash and drain. ❧ Heat oil and deep-fry fish until golden brown. Drain and set aside. ❧ Heat 3 tablespoons oil and sauté ground spices until fragrant, then add lemon grass, tamarind juice and sweet soy sauce. When the sauce has thickened, spread it over deep-fried fish.

Opposite: (From left) Ikan Bumbu Bali and Pindang Serani

Pecak Lele

(Grilled Fish in Hot Sauce)

~

2–3	catfish (600 grams)
1	teaspoon tamarind
$^1/_2$	teaspoon salt
250	cc coconut milk from $^1/_2$ coconut
25	grams basil leaves

Spices (ground):

3	red chillies, steamed or grilled
5	bird's eye chillies, steamed or grilled
2	teaspoons chopped lesser galangal, roasted
3	candlenuts, fried
2	kaffir lime leaves, fried
	salt and sugar / brown sugar

Clean and gut catfish, then score the sides. Rub with tamarind and salt, and let it stand for 10 minutes. ❧ Grill the fish over hot charcoal until it is cooked. Press the fish with the back of a spoon so that the spices will be easily absorbed. ❧ Mix the ground spices with coconut milk. Allow to simmer and stir from time to time until the milk boils. Add basil leaves. Remove from heat and pour over grilled fish.

Note: You can use steamed banana buds or pink ginger buds instead of catfish.

Pepes Ikan Mas

(Grilled Carp)

~

1	carp (750 grams)
1	lime, extract juice
$1^1/_2$	teaspoons salt
10	cm turmeric, thinly sliced
3	cm galangal, thinly sliced
5	*salam* leaves (or bay leaves as a substitute)
3	stalks lemon grass, halved, bruised
7	shallots, thinly sliced
3	cloves garlic, thinly sliced
2	red chillies, sliced coarsely
10	bird's eye chillies
25	grams basil leaves
2	tomatoes, chopped
	banana leaves

Clean and gut fish and remove scales. Cut off the fins and gills, then rinse the fish under running water. Score the sides, then rub with lime juice and $^1/_2$ teaspoon salt. Let it stand for 30 minutes. ❧ Mix the other ingredients with 1 teaspoon salt and rub it on the fish. Wrap the spiced fish with banana leaves and tie both ends. ❧ Grill over hot charcoal or bake in an oven until cooked and dry.

Opposite: (From left) Pepes Ikan Mas and Pecak Lele

Sate Ikan

(Fish and Glass Noodles in Banana Leaf)
~

500	grams fish fillet, minced
25	grams glass noodles, cut into 10 cm lengths, soaked in water until tender, drained
1	onion, chopped
$^1/_2$	teaspoon pepper
1	teaspoon salt
200	cc thick coconut milk from 1 coconut banana leaves

Mix all ingredients thoroughly. ❧ Put 1–2 tablespoons fish mixture on a banana leaf and wrap. Do the same for the remaining mixture. ❧ Steam until cooked. Remove from steamer and serve.

Pindang Kecap

(Milkfish in Sweet Soy Sauce)
~

1	cm turmeric
1	cm ginger
2	cm galangal
1	milkfish (700 grams)
1	teaspoon tamarind juice
$^1/_2$	teaspoon salt
500	cc water
2	*salam* leaves (or bay leaves as a substitute)
1	stalk lemon grass, bruised
3	tablespoons sweet soy sauce
5	unpeeled shallots, roasted, peeled, thinly sliced
3	cloves unpeeled garlic, roasted, peeled, thinly sliced
1–2	tablespoons tamarind juice
5	carambolas, halved
10	bird's eye chillies
2	red chillies, cut into 2 cm pieces
	salt and brown sugar

Thread turmeric, ginger and galangal onto a skewer and grill. Set aside. ❧ Clean the fish, remove scales and cut off the fins and gills. Cut into 4–5 pieces. Rub with tamarind and salt, and let it stand for 15 minutes. Drain. ❧ Bring water to the boil, and add grilled turmeric, ginger and galangal, *salam* leaves, lemon grass, sweet soy sauce, shallots and garlic. Add fish, tamarind juice, carambolas, chillies, salt and sugar. Continue to cook over low heat until the spices are absorbed before serving.

Opposite: (From left) Sate Ikan and Pindang Kecap

Sepat Banang
(Milkfish with Mango and Prawns)
~

1	milkfish / other fish (500 grams)
	lime juice
	salt
200	grams prawns, discard the head
1	mango (300 grams), peeled and
	cut into long strips
200	cc coconut milk from ¹/₂ coconut
1–2	tablespoons lime juice
25	grams basil leaves

Spices (ground):

5	bird's eye chillies
4	shallots, roasted, peeled
3	candlenuts, roasted / fried
	salt and sugar / brown sugar

Clean and gut fish and remove scales, gills, and fins. Rub with lime juice and salt. Wash and drain. ❧ Squeeze the mango slices with salt until tender, then rinse and drain. ❧ Grill the prawns and fish over hot charcoal until cooked. ❧ Combine ground spices, coconut milk, fish and prawns with mango and lime juice. Mix well. Garnish with basil leaves.

Optional: Fish may also be served simply grilled, without the coconut milk sauce.

Panggang Haruan
(Grilled Catfish Stuffed with Chilli)
~

2	(650 grams) fresh catfish
5	shallots, ground
¹/₂	teaspoon minced turmeric, ground
¹/₂	teaspoon salt
1	tablespoon margarine, melted
6	tablespoons oil

Spices (ground):

10	red chillies
7	shallots
3	cloves garlic
¹/₂	shrimp paste
2	tomatoes, chopped

Clean fish and remove scales, gills, entrails, fins and head. Make a slit along the underside of the fish right down to the tail, without cutting the tail off. ❧ Rub fish with shallots, turmeric and salt. Stuff the fish with some of the ground spices. Grill it over hot charcoal or bake in an oven, at intervals brushing with melted margarine until cooked. ❧ Heat oil and sauté remaining ground spices until fragrant, then pour over the fish.

Opposite: (From left) Sepat Banang (fish and prawns) and Panggang Haruan

Sate Bandeng
(Grilled Stuffed Milkfish)
~

1	fresh milkfish (600 grams)
3	tablespoons oil
1/3	coconut, roasted, coarsely pounded
1	egg, lightly beaten
	banana leaf
125	cc thick coconut milk from 1 coconut
	salt

Spices (ground):

2–3	red chillies
2	teaspoons coriander, roasted
1/2	teaspoon cumin
1	teaspoon chopped ginger
2	teaspoons chopped galangal
1	teaspoon chopped turmeric
5	shallots
5	cloves garlic
1	teaspoon tamarind juice
	salt and sugar / brown sugar

Clean fish and remove scales, fins, gills and entrails. Rinse and pat it dry. Pound the fish lightly until the flesh becomes tender. Using a small sharp knife, remove the backbone and as much of the flesh as possible through a slit under the gills, taking care not to break the skin. Set the skin aside. ❖ Roast the flesh until it changes colour, then discard the bones and grind the flesh. ❖ Heat oil and sauté ground spices until fragrant. Remove and allow to cool. Combine the sautéed spices with ground fish, pounded coconut and egg. ❖ Stuff the fish skin with this mixture. Make a slit in a bamboo stick and clamp the stuffed skin with the slit bamboo. Tie both ends of the stick. Wrap the fish with banana leaf and grill until fish is firm. ❖ Remove the banana leaf and continue to grill. Brush fish with salted thick coconut milk from time to time until it is cooked. Remove fish from heat and cut before serving.

Note: In East Java, Sate Bandeng is called Otak-Otak Bandeng (Grilled / Fried Fish Mixture). The fish is not brushed with thick coconut milk while grilling. Instead, it is fried / baked until cooked. The filling is made up of mashed potatoes.

Ikan Mas Woku
(Carp in Herbal Curry)
~

1	(850 grams) carp
1	lime, extract juice
5	tablespoons oil
5	kaffir lime leaves, thinly sliced
1	turmeric leaf, thinly sliced
1/2	pandanus leaf, thinly sliced
250	cc water
3	cumin leaves, thinly sliced (if available)
2	spring onions, coarsely chopped
25	grams basil leaves

Spices (ground):

5	red chillies
50	grams bird's eye chillies (use less if you prefer)
2	teaspoons chopped turmeric
2	teaspoons chopped ginger
3–4	tomatoes
10	candlenuts / almonds, roasted
1	tablespoon thinly sliced lemon grass
1	teaspoon salt

Clean and wash fish. Rub with lime juice and let it stand for 10 minutes. ❖ Heat oil and sauté ground spices and kaffir lime, turmeric and pandanus leaves until fragrant. Add water and bring to the boil. ❖ Toss in the fish and continue to cook over low heat. Add cumin leaves and spring onions. Simmer until cooked. When the sauce is completely absorbed, adjust seasoning if necessary then add basil leaves. Remove from heat and serve.

Opposite: (From left) Ikan Mas Woku and Sate Bandeng

Arsik

(Carp Stuffed with Herbs and Spices)

~

1	(850 grams) carp
	salt and lime juice
10	stalks lemon grass, bruised
2	pink ginger buds, each cut into 2–4 pieces
3	pieces *asam gelugur*
5	cup leaves, coarsely sliced
10	stalks Chinese chives
1	tablespoon tamarind, soaked in 250 cc water, squeeze the pulp and strain the juice

Spices (ground):

10	red chillies
1	tablespoon Szechuan pepper
7	candlenuts, roasted
2	teaspoons chopped ginger
2	teaspoons chopped turmeric
1	tablespoon chopped young galangal
10	shallots
3	cloves garlic
2	teaspoons salt

Clean fish and remove scales, entrails, gills and fins. Wash and drain. Rub fish with salt and lime juice, and let it stand for 10 minutes. ❧ Stuff fish with some of the ground spices, lemon grass and pink ginger buds. Rub the whole fish with remaining ground spices. ❧ Put fish, *asam gelugur*, cup leaves and Chinese chives in a pan and pour tamarind juice. ❧ Simmer uncovered until the fish is cooked and the gravy has thickened. ❧ During cooking, you may add 15 whole string beans or 250 grams sour bamboo shoots.

Udang Pedas

(Spicy Prawns and Green Beans)

~

2	tablespoons oil
350	grams medium-sized prawns, discard the head
100	grams Chinese chives
15	green beans (*petai*)
1	tablespoon lime juice

Spices (ground):

100	grams red chillies
1	tomato
5	shallots
2	cloves garlic
1	teaspoon salt

Heat oil and sauté ground spices. Add prawns, Chinese chives and *petai*. Stir frequently, taking care not to overcook the prawns. ❧ Add lime juice before removing from heat.

Opposite: (From left) Udang Pedas and Arsik

Sate Lilit
(Minced Fish Satay)
~

3	tablespoons oil
500	grams fish fillet
5	tablespoons shredded coconut
50	cc thick coconut milk
5	kaffir lime leaves, thinly sliced
	a few stalks of lemon grass / satay skewers

Spices (ground):

4	red chillies
4	bird's eye chillies
1	teaspoon lesser galangal
1/2	teaspoon chopped galangal
1/2	teaspoon turmeric
3	candlenuts, roasted
1/2	tablespoon sliced lemon grass
2	cloves garlic
5	shallots
	salt and sugar / brown sugar

Heat oil and sauté ground spices until fragrant. Remove from heat and allow to cool. ✏ Finely chop fish fillet and combine with shredded coconut, three-quarters of the thick coconut milk, sautéed spices and kaffir lime leaves. Stir and mix thoroughly. ✏ Shape 2 tablespoons fish mixture around a satay skewer or stalk of lemon grass. Press firmly until it sticks to the skewer or stalk. ✏ Grill the skewered fish over hot charcoal and brush with remaining coconut milk until cooked.

Japit Udang
(Prawn Satay)
~

20	large prawns, peeled, leaving the tail
100	cc thick coconut milk
	bamboo skewers and banana leaf stalks

Spices (ground):

8–10	red chillies
1	teaspoon chopped lesser galangal
5	candlenuts, roasted
6	shallots
3	cloves garlic
	salt and sugar / brown sugar

Combine prawns with ground spices and thick coconut milk and allow to stand for 15 minutes. ✏ Clamp 4–5 prawns between a skewer which is split into two along the middle. Tie one end with a banana leaf stalk. ✏ Grill over hot charcoal and brush with remaining ground spices until golden brown.

Mangut Ikan Pe
(Fish and Chayote in Coconut Milk)
~

300	cc thin coconut milk
1	chayote, cut into 2 cm cubes
200	grams grilled baby shark
50	grams string beans, cut into 3 cm pieces
50	grams melinjo leaves
10	green beans (*petai*)
3	green chillies, sliced across
5	red chillies, sliced across
2	cm galangal, bruised
2	*salam* leaves (or bay leaves as a substitute)
	salt and sugar
200	cc thick coconut milk

Spices (ground):

5	shallots
2	cloves garlic
1/2	teaspoon chopped lesser galangal
1/2	teaspoon shrimp paste

Bring to the boil thin coconut milk with ground spices. Add chayote and fish. ✏ Allow to simmer until the chayote is soft. Add all other ingredients except thick coconut milk, stir well and continue to cook. ✏ When vegetables are nearly cooked, add thick coconut milk and keep stirring from time to time to prevent coconut milk from curdling.

Opposite: Mangut Ikan Pe and (on a plate,
from left) Sate Lilit and Japit Udang

Pelas Udang

(Spiced Shrimps Grilled in Banana Leaf)

~

500   grams shrimps, shelled and chopped
1/2   coconut, shredded
      banana leaves

Spices (ground):

5   red chillies (discard the seeds if you
    do not like it hot)
2   teaspoons coriander, roasted
3   kaffir lime leaves
3   cloves garlic
7   shallots
2   teaspoons chopped galangal
4   candlenuts, fried
1   teaspoon tamarind juice
2   teaspoons salt and sugar / brown sugar

Combine chopped shrimps with shredded coconut and ground spices. Mix well. ❧ Wrap 1 1/2 tablespoons of the mixture with banana leaf. Roll the leaf up and secure both ends with toothpicks. Continue to wrap until all the mixture is used up. ❧ Grill over hot charcoal or bake in an oven until cooked.

Tumis Udang

(Stir-fried Prawns in Coconut Gravy)

~

500   grams medium-sized prawns, discard the head
1   tablespoon lime juice
1/2   teaspoon salt
1/4   teaspoon pepper
3   tablespoons oil
1   lemon grass, bruised
1/2   pandanus leaf
2   cm cinnamon
1   cardamom
250   cc coconut milk
5   curry leaves
1   clove
5   green chillies
6   carambolas, sliced across 1/2 cm thick

Spices (ground):

5   red chillies
1   teaspoon coriander
1/2   teaspoon peppercorns, roasted
1/6   teaspoon cumin
1/2   tablespoon dried carambola
3   cloves garlic
6   shallots
1   teaspoon chopped ginger
1   teaspoon chopped turmeric

Rub prawns with lime juice, salt and pepper, and allow to stand for 10 minutes. ❧ Heat oil and sauté ground spices, lemon grass, pandanus leaf, cinnamon and cardamom. Add prawns, coconut milk and other ingredients. ❧ Simmer over low heat until the gravy thickens.

Rajungan Goreng

(Chilli Crabs)

~

1   kg medium-sized crabs
1   tablespoon lime juice
1   egg, lightly beaten
    oil for deep-frying

Spices (ground):

1–2   red chillies
1/2   teaspoon salt
2   cloves garlic
1/2   teaspoon chopped ginger
1/2   teaspoon pepper

Clean crabs, discard the shell and gills, and twist off the legs and claws. ❧ Cut in half if the crab is too big. Add lime juice and let it stand for 10 minutes. ❧ Combine ground spices with egg, add the crabs and mix well. Heat oil and deep-fry crabs until golden brown.

Opposite: (Clockwise from top) Rajungan Goreng,
Tumis Udang and Pelas Udang

Kare Kepiting
(Crab Curry)
~

5	crabs
3	tablespoons oil
1	stalk lemon grass, bruised
1	*salam* leaf (or bay leaf as a substitute)
2	kaffir lime leaves
1	litre coconut from 1 coconut
	salt

Spices (ground):

4	red chillies
1	teaspoon chopped ginger
1	teaspoon chopped turmeric
2	teaspoons chopped galangal
1	teaspoon coriander, roasted
3	candlenuts, roasted
1/6	teaspoon cumin, roasted
1/4	teaspoon shrimp paste
2	cloves garlic
5	shallots
1	teaspoon tamarind juice

Clean crabs and discard the shell and gills. Cut in half. Heat oil and sauté ground spices, lemon grass, *salam* leaf and kaffir lime leaves until fragrant. Add coconut milk and salt and bring to the boil. Toss in the crabs and simmer until cooked.

Tumis Nus
(Stir-fried Squid)
~

750	grams squid
1	tablespoon lime juice / tamarind juice
1/2	teaspoon salt
5	tablespoons oil
2	*salam* leaves (or bay leaves as a substitute)
3	red chillies, seeded, thinly sliced
250	cc stock
50	grams basil leaves
	salt
	fried shallots, for garnishing

Spices (ground):

7	red chillies
10	bird's eye chillies
5	candlenuts, roasted
1/2	teaspoon chopped lesser galangal
1	teaspoon chopped turmeric
2	teaspoons chopped galangal
1	tablespoon thinly sliced lemon grass
1/2	teaspoon chopped ginger
3	cloves garlic
8	shallots
1/2	teaspoon shrimp paste

Wash squid and peel off the reddish-brown membrane. Remove the head and discard the ink bag and transparent white spine. Cut out the stone just behind the eye and discard. Rinse and drain. ❧ Rub squid with lime or tamarind juice and salt, and let it stand for 15 minutes. ❧ Heat oil and sauté ground spices and *salam* leaves until fragrant. Then add chillies and squid. Continue to stir until the spices are absorbed. Add the stock and cook until the gravy thickens. Add basil leaves, then reduce heat and continue to cook. Garnish with fried shallots.

Note: When using fresh squid, the ink bag can be kept if you prefer the sauce to be dark.

Opposite: (From left) Tumis Nus and Kare Kepiting

Sambal Kerang

(Cockles in Spiced Shredded Coconut)
~

500	grams fresh cockles
1	turmeric leaf, torn and knotted
5	kaffir lime leaves
1–2	pieces *asam gelugur*
500	cc coconut milk from 1 coconut
$1/2$	coconut, shredded

Spices (ground):

100	grams red chillies
4	cloves garlic
8	shallots
1	tablespoon thinly sliced lemon grass
2	teaspoons chopped ginger
2	teaspoons chopped turmeric
1	tablespoon chopped galangal
2	teaspoons coriander, roasted
$1/6$	teaspoon cumin, roasted
$1^1/2$	teaspoons salt

Put the cockles in a pan and add ground spices, turmeric and kaffir lime leaves, *asam gelugur* and coconut milk. ◦ Cook until the cockles are soft and the gravy has thickened. Add shredded coconut and continue cooking until the coconut is dry and golden brown.

Sambal Tuk-tuk

(Shredded Salted Fish with Green Beans)
~

250	grams salted fish (catfish or any small fish)
10	tablespoons oil
15	green beans (*petai*), halved
75	grams pea aubergines
1–2	limes, extract juice

Spices (ground):

100	grams red chillies
7	shallots
	salt

Grill salted fish then wash. Pound the flesh until tender and discard the bone. (If you are using a small fish, roast it then discard the head and pound until tender.) ◦ Heat oil and sauté ground spices. Add *petai* and pea aubergines. Simmer until almost cooked, then toss in the fish and add lime juice.

Sambal Udang

(Prawns in Chilli and Candlenut Gravy)
~

500	grams large prawns, remove the head
1	tablespoon lime juice
3	tablespoons oil
2	*salam* leaves (or bay leaves as a substitute)
125	cc water / thin coconut milk
	fried shallots
1	tablespoon thinly sliced orange peel

Spices (ground):

7–8	red chillies
10	bird's eye chillies (optional)
2	cloves garlic
6	shallots
$1/2$	teaspoon chopped turmeric
1	teaspoon chopped ginger
$1/2$	teaspoon shrimp paste
1	tablespoon sliced lemon grass
1	teaspoon coriander, roasted
1–2	teaspoons tamarind juice
5	candlenuts, roasted / fried
	salt and brown sugar

Knead prawns with lime juice and let it stand for 10 minutes. ◦ Heat oil and sauté ground spices and *salam* leaves until fragrant, then pour in water or thin coconut milk. Bring to the boil, then add prawns. Cook until the gravy has thickened. ◦ Garnish with fried shallots and orange peel.

Opposite: (From top) Sambal Udang,
Sambal Kerang and Sambal Tuk-tuk

Palai Bada

(Whitebait and Herbs Grilled in Banana Leaf)

500	grams fresh whitebait, discard the head
1/2	coconut, shredded, finely pounded
4	cup leaves, thinly sliced
1/2	turmeric leaf, thinly sliced
25	grams sliced basil leaves
	banana leaves

Spices (ground):

8	red chillies
7	shallots
1	teaspoon chopped ginger
1	teaspoon chopped turmeric
1	tablespoon sliced lemon grass
1	lime, extract the pulp

Rinse fish, then drain. Combine shredded coconut, ground spices, whitebait, sliced cup, turmeric and basil leaves and mix well. ❧ Put 1–2 tablespoons fish mixture on 1 banana leaf, roll up and secure both ends with toothpicks. Repeat this process with the remaining mixture. Grill over hot charcoal until cooked.

Note: You can substitute whitebait with the same amount of peeled small shrimps.

Sop Tekwan

(Fish Ball Soup)

250	grams shrimps, shelled, finely chopped (reserve shells for stock)
1 1/2	litres water
2	tablespoons margarine
25	grams mushrooms, soaked in hot water
25	dried lily buds, soaked in hot water until tender, knotted
1	(250 grams) yam bean, cut into strips 1/2 x 1/2 x 5 cm
	salt
3	spring onions, thinly sliced
2	sprigs Chinese parsley, coarsely sliced
	fried shallots

Fish Balls:

250	grams fish fillet (Spanish mackerel / snapper)
175	grams corn starch
25	grams flour
1	egg white
1 1/2	teaspoons salt
100	cc water
	seasoning

Spices (ground):

6	cloves garlic
1	teaspoon peppercorns

Stock: Roast shrimp shells until they turn red. Add 1 1/2 litres water, bring to the boil and simmer for 1/2 hour. Strain the stock, reduce heat and continue to cook until the stock boils.

Fish Balls: Mix ingredients for fish balls. Shape a teaspoon of mixture into balls and toss into boiling water until just cooked.

Heat margarine and sauté ground spices. Add shrimps, mushrooms, lily buds and yam bean. Continue to fry until soft. Add to the shrimp stock. Before removing from heat, add fish balls, salt, spring onion and parsley. Garnish with fried shallots and serve with chilli sauce.

Opposite: (From left) Palai Bada and Sop Tekwan

SOYBEAN

168 *Tempe Panggang Bumbu Rujak*

Grilled Spiced Fermented Soybean
—Java

Sambal Tempe Teri Kacang

Fried Fermented Soybean with Whitebait and Peanuts—Sumatra

Mendoan

Fried Spiced Fermented Soybean
—Central Java

170 *Kering Tempe*

Fried Fermented Soybean—Java

Terik Tempe dan Tahu

Fried Spiced Fermented Soybean and Bean Curd—Central Java

Tumis Tempe Santan Kecap

Fermented Soybean and Green Beans in Coconut Milk—Central Java

172 *Perkedel Tempe / Medol*

Fermented Soybean Croquettes
—Central & East Java

Orem-Orem

Stewed Fermented Soybean
—Malang, East Java

Sambal Tumpang

Fermented Soybean in Bone Soup
—Central Java

174 *Pepes Oncom*

Fermented Soybean Waste Grilled in Banana Leaf—West Java

Tumis Oncom

Fried Fermented Soybean Waste
—West Java

Sambal Oncom

Grilled Fermented Soybean Waste in Chilli—West Java

176 *Tahu Lengko*

Bean Curd with Peanut Sauce
—Cirebon, West Java

Gadon Tahu

Steamed Bean Curd and Egg
—Central Java

178 *Tahu Gimbal*

Bean Curd with Shrimp Fritters
—Central Java

Tahu Campur

Bean Curd and Dried Noodles Soup
—East Java

180 *Tahu Telur*

Bean Curd Fried in Eggs with Peanut Sauce—East Java

Tahu Isi

Bean Curd Stuffed with Chicken and Shrimps—Central & East Java

182 *Tahu Berontak*

Fried Stuffed Bean Curd
—Central Java

Tahu Gejrot

Fried Bean Curd with Sweet-Sour Sauce—Cirebon, West Java

Tempe Panggang Bumbu Rujak

(Grilled Spiced Fermented Soybean)
~

1	piece fermented soybean (350 grams)
2	tablespoons oil
1	stalk lemon grass, bruised
2	kaffir lime leaves
250	cc coconut milk from 1/2 coconut

Spices (ground):

5	red chillies
3	candlenuts, roasted
5	shallots
2	cloves garlic
1/2	teaspoon shrimp paste
1/2	teaspoon tamarind
1/2	tablespoon chopped galangal
	salt and sugar

Score the sides of the fermented soybean, then steam for 15 minutes. ᚛ Heat oil and sauté lemon grass, kaffir lime leaves and ground spices until fragrant. Then add coconut milk, toss in the fermented soybean and continue to cook until the gravy thickens. ᚛ Remove the fermented soybean and brush it with the sautéed spices. Grill over hot charcoal until the fermented soybean is almost dry. Set aside and cut. Serve with the remaining sautéed spices.

Sambal Tempe Teri Kacang

(Fried Fermented Soybean with Whitebait and Peanuts)
~

250	grams fermented soybean, thinly sliced 1/2 x 3 cm, deep-fried until crispy
5	tablespoons oil
50	grams whitebait, washed and fried
100	grams peanuts, fried, drained
1	lime, extract juice

Spices (ground):

10	red chillies
5	shallots
2	cloves garlic
	salt

Heat oil and sauté ground spices until fragrant. Toss in the fermented soybean, whitebait and peanuts, then add lime juice. Mix well and serve.

Mendoan

(Fried Spiced Fermented Soybean)
~

1	piece fermented soybean (300 grams)
75	grams rice flour
1	tablespoon cornstarch
125	cc coconut milk
5	Chinese chives, cut into 1 cm pieces
	oil for deep-frying

Spices (ground):

3	candlenuts, roasted
2	cloves garlic
1/2	teaspoon coriander, roasted
1/2	teaspoon lesser galangal, roasted
1/2	teaspoon salt

Slice fermented soybean into pieces 1/2 x 5 x 7 cm. ᚛ Mix ground spices, rice flour and cornstarch. Add coconut milk and mix until smooth, then add Chinese chives. ᚛ Dip fermented soybean one slice at a time into the mixture, then deep-fry until golden brown. Drain and serve with sweet soy sauce and sliced bird's eye chillies.

Note: This dish comes from Banyumas and Purwokerto in Central Java, where it is usually sold as thinly sliced soybean cakes wrapped in banana leaves. If you are using this type of fermented soybean, fry until it is half-cooked.

Opposite: (Clockwise from top) Tempe Panggang Bumbu Rujak, Mendoan, Kering Tempe (page 170) and Sambal Tempe Teri Kacang

Kering Tempe
(Fried Fermented Soybean)
~

1	piece fermented soybean (300 grams)
	oil for deep-frying
100	grams peanuts
5	red chillies, seeded, sliced diagonally
5	tablespoons oil
3	cloves garlic, ground
1	tablespoon ground galangal
1	*salam* leaf (or bay leaf as a substitute)
1	teaspoon tamarind, soaked in water, squeeze the pulp and strain the juice
50	grams brown sugar
	salt
50	grams shallots, sliced and fried

Cut the fermented soybean thinly into pieces 1 x 1 x 4 cm. Deep-fry in oil until crispy and golden brown. Fry peanuts until brown, then set aside. Fry sliced chillies until crispy and set aside. ❧ With 5 tablespoons oil, sauté ground garlic and galangal and *salam* leaf until fragrant. Add tamarind juice, brown sugar and salt. Reduce heat and continue to cook until the sauce has thickened. Add fermented soybean, fried peanuts, chillies and fried shallots. Stir well. Remove from heat. When cool, store in an airtight jar.

Terik Tempe dan Tahu
(Fried Spiced Fermented Soybean and Bean Curd)
~

5	pieces bean curd (5 x 5 cm)
2	tablespoons oil
3	kaffir lime leaves
500	cc coconut milk
300	grams fermented soybean, cut into pieces 2 x 3 x 4 cm

Spices (ground):

1	teaspoon peppercorns
1	teaspoon coriander, roasted
3	candlenuts, roasted
2	cloves garlic
5	shallots
2	teaspoons chopped galangal
	salt and brown sugar

Fry bean curd until half-cooked, then set aside. ❧ Sauté ground spices and kaffir lime leaves until fragrant. Add coconut milk and bring to the boil. Toss in fermented soybean and bean curd. Simmer over low heat until the gravy has thickened. Remove from heat and serve.

Note: The dish looks brownish because brown sugar is used.

Tumis Tempe Santan Kecap
(Fermented Soybean and Green Beans in Coconut Milk)
~

300	grams fermented soybean
3	tablespoons oil
7	shallots, finely sliced
3	cloves garlic, finely sliced
5	green chillies, sliced into 1 cm pieces
2	red chillies, sliced into 1 cm pieces
1	*salam* leaf (or bay leaf as a substitute)
1	cm galangal, bruised
2	tomatoes, each cut into 4–6 pieces
500	cc coconut milk
3	tablespoons sweet soy sauce
1	teaspoon salt
2	teaspoons brown sugar
15	green beans (*petai*), halved
200	grams shrimps

Cut fermented soybean into 1 cm cubes. Fry until half-cooked then drain. ❧ Sauté shallots and garlic until fragrant. Add chillies, *salam* leaf, galangal and tomatoes. Stir until the ingredients are soft. Then add fermented soybean, coconut milk, sweet soy sauce, salt and sugar. ❧ Add *petai* and shrimps. Simmer until the sauce has thickened.

Opposite: (Clockwise from top) Terik Tempe dan Tahu, Tumis Tempe Santan Kecap and Perkedel Tempe / Medol (page 172)

Perkedel Tempe / Medol

(Fermented Soybean Croquettes)
~

1	piece fermented soybean (300 grams), finely ground
	oil for deep-frying

Spices (ground):

5–10	bird's eye chillies
2	cloves garlic
2	shallots
1	teaspoon chopped lesser galangal
3	kaffir lime leaves
1	teaspoon salt

Combine ground fermented soybean with ground spices and mix thoroughly. ⮞ Shape the mixture into balls, then flatten slightly. Deep-fry in hot oil until golden brown.

Orem-Orem

(Stewed Fermented Soybean)
~

500	cc coconut milk
2	tablespoons dried shrimps
1	*salam* leaf (or bay leaf as a substitute)
2	kaffir lime leaves
1	cm galangal, bruised
300	grams fermented soybean, cut into pieces 2 x 3 cm
50	grams green chillies, coarsely sliced
2	spring onions, cut into 2 cm lengths

Spices (ground):

1/2	teaspoon chopped lesser galangal
1	teaspoon chopped coriander leaves
1/2	teaspoon chopped turmeric
2	cloves garlic
5	shallots

Bring to the boil coconut milk with dried shrimps, ground spices, *salam* and kaffir lime leaves and galangal. ⮞ Add fermented soybean, green chillies and spring onions. Simmer until the gravy has thickened.

Sambal Tumpang

(Fermented Soybean in Bone Soup)
~

250	grams fermented soybean
250	grams over-fermented soybean
7	shallots
3	cloves garlic
5	red chillies
5	bird's eye chillies
1 1/2	teaspoons chopped lesser galangal
200	grams offal
2	*salam* leaves (or bay leaves as a substitute)
2	cm galangal, bruised
2	kaffir lime leaves
25	grams dried shrimps
500	cc coconut milk
1–2	teaspoons salt
2	teaspoons brown sugar
75	grams crackled water buffalo rind

Steam fermented and over-fermented soybean with shallots, garlic, chillies and lesser galangal. Grind until very fine. ⮞ Boil offal with enough water to cover until offal is tender. Remove offal and reserve 750 cc stock. ⮞ Add ground soybean mixture to the stock with *salam* leaves, galangal, kaffir lime leaves and dried shrimps and bring to the boil. Then add coconut milk, salt, brown sugar and buffalo rind. Continue to cook until the sauce thickens.

Over-fermented Soybean: Rinse 1 piece fresh fermented soybean and rub with salt. Wrap in a banana leaf, and let it stand overnight in a warm place.

Note: Sambal Tumpang is usually eaten with mixed vegetables consisting of shredded and steamed young papaya.

Opposite: (From top) Sambal Tumpang and Orem-Orem

Pepes Oncom
(Fermented Soybean Waste Grilled in Banana Leaf)
~

2	pieces fermented soybean waste (2 x 8 x 10 cm)
5	tablespoons hot water
5	green chillies, coarsely sliced
6	red chillies, coarsely sliced
10	bird's eye chillies
4	spring onions, finely sliced
25	grams basil leaves
8	*salam* leaves (or bay leaves as a substitute)
	banana leaves, for wrapping

Spices (ground):

8	shallots
4	cloves garlic
1½	teaspoons chopped ginger
1	teaspoon shrimp paste
	salt and sugar

Grind fermented soybean waste. Combine with ground spices, hot water, chillies, spring onions and basil leaves. Mix well and divide into 8 portions. ❧ Take 2 banana leaves, add 1 *salam* or bay leaf and 1 portion of the mixture. Wrap the banana leaves and secure both ends. Steam for 30 minutes or until cooked. ❧ Roast for a few minutes until dry, then serve.

Tumis Oncom
(Fried Fermented Soybean Waste)
~

3	tablespoons oil
8	shallots, finely sliced
3	cloves garlic, finely sliced
3	green chillies, finely sliced
2	red chillies, finely sliced
10	bird's eye chillies
3	*salam* leaves (or bay leaves as a substitute)
1	piece galangal, bruised
25	grams dried shrimps
2	pieces fermented soybean waste (2 x 8 x 10 cm), rinsed and ground
100	grams *leunca*
2–3	teaspoons ground chilli
	salt and sugar

Heat oil and sauté shallots and garlic until fragrant. Add chillies, *salam* leaves, galangal, dried shrimps and fermented soybean waste. Mix thoroughly. Add some water and allow to simmer until the sauce thickens. Add *leunca* and ground chilli. Cook until the sauce is almost absorbed, and season with salt and sugar.

Sambal Oncom
(Grilled Fermented Soybean Waste in Chilli)
~

1	piece fermented soybean waste (3 x 8 x 12 cm), grilled
2	teaspoons chopped lesser galangal
1	teaspoon chopped ginger
3	cloves garlic
1–2	teaspoons shrimp paste
10	bird's eye chillies
3	red chillies
	salt and brown sugar
1	teaspoon tamarind juice
5–6	tablespoons water

Grind roasted fermented soybean waste. ❧ Grind lesser galangal with ginger, garlic, shrimp paste, chillies and salt and sugar until fine. Combine with ground fermented soybean waste and tamarind juice. Add some water and mix thoroughly. Serve with raw or steamed vegetables.

Opposite: (Clockwise from left) Sambal Oncom, Pepes Oncom and Tumis Oncom

Tahu Lengko
(Bean Curd with Peanut Sauce)
~

2	pieces large bean curd (8 x 8 cm), halved and fried
1	piece fermented soybean (300 grams), cut into 2–3 pieces, fried
2	cucumbers, quartered, cut into 1 cm pieces
200	grams bean sprouts, tailed, blanched, drained
1–2	tablespoons fried shallots
4	sprigs Chinese chives, cut into 1 cm pieces
3–4	tablespoons sweet soy sauce

Peanut Sauce:

150	grams peanuts, fried and ground
2	red chillies, ground
10	bird's eye chillies, ground
150	cc water
$1/2$	teaspoon salt

Cut fried bean curd and fermented soybean into 1 cm cubes. Set aside. Combine all the ingredients for peanut sauce and mix well. ☙ Arrange bean curd, fermented soybean, cucumber and bean sprouts on a serving plate. Pour peanut sauce over, and garnish with fried shallots, Chinese chives and sweet soy sauce.

Gadon Tahu
(Steamed Bean Curd and Egg)
~

6	pieces small or 2 pieces large bean curd, ground
1	egg, lightly beaten
5	tablespoons thick coconut milk
	salam leaves (or bay leaves as a substitute)
	banana leaves, for wrapping

Spices (ground):

1	teaspoon coriander
$1/8$	teaspoon cumin, roasted
3	candlenuts
$1/2$	teaspoon peppercorns
2	cloves garlic
4	shallots
	salt and brown sugar

Mix ground bean curd with ground spices, beaten egg and coconut milk. ☙ On a banana leaf, put 1 *salam* or bay leaf and 1–2 tablespoons bean curd mixture. Wrap in a pyramid-like shape, and secure the top with toothpick. Steam until cooked.

Opposite: (From top) Gadon Tahu and Tahu Lengko

Tahu Gimbal
(Bean Curd with Shrimp Fritters)
~

2   pieces large bean curd (8 x 8 x 2 cm),
     quartered
     oil for deep-frying
4   cabbage leaves, finely sliced

Shrimp Fritters:
100   grams flour
1/4   teaspoon baking soda
1   egg, beaten
2   teaspoons salt
1   clove garlic, ground
1/4   teaspoon pepper
100   grams bean sprouts, tailed
200   grams shrimps, discard the head
1   tablespoon chopped Chinese parsley
125   cc water / thin coconut milk
      oil for deep-frying

Peanut Sauce:
2–3   tablespoons sweet soy sauce
125   cc water

Spices (ground):
150   grams peanuts, roasted and peeled
2–3   shallots
10   bird's eye chillies
1/2   teaspoon salt
1   teaspoon sugar

Deep-fry bean curd until golden brown, then set aside.

Shrimp Fritters: Combine flour with baking soda, egg, salt, garlic and pepper. Mix well. Add bean sprouts, shrimps, Chinese parsley and coconut milk. Deep-fry 1–2 tablespoons of the mixture until golden brown. Drain and set aside.

Peanut Sauce: Combine sweet soy sauce with water and ground spices. Mix thoroughly.

How to Serve: Cut bean curd and shrimp fritters into serving pieces. Arrange on a serving plate, add sliced cabbage, and pour the peanut sauce over.

Tahu Campur
(Bean Curd and Dried Noodles Soup)
~

3   tablespoons oil
3   pieces large bean curd, fried and cut into
     pieces 1 x 1 x 2 cm
7–8 lettuce leaves
150 grams dried noodles, blanched, drained
150 grams bean sprouts, tailed, blanched, drained
200 grams potatoes, boiled, sliced
     shallots and garlic, sliced and fried

Spices (ground):
2   teaspoons coriander
1/4   teaspoon cumin, roasted
1   teaspoon peppercorns
7   shallots
3   cloves garlic
      salt and sugar

Soup:
2   *salam* leaves (or bay leaves as a substitute)
2   cm ginger, bruised
2   cm galangal, bruised
1 1/2 litres meat stock
250   grams offal, boiled until tender,
      cut into pieces 1 x 1 cm

Soup: Heat oil and sauté ground spices, *salam* leaves, ginger and galangal until fragrant. Add to the stock together with offal and bring to the boil.

Lento: Combine 250 grams shredded cassava and 1 clove garlic with 1 teaspoon coriander. Grind until fine, then shape into balls (like croquettes). Deep-fry until golden brown.

Sambal Petis (Black Shrimp Paste Sauce): Grind 5 bird's eye chillies with 1–2 tablespoons black shrimp paste. Add 2 tablespoons water. Mix thoroughly.

How to Serve: Arrange bean curd, lettuce leaves, noodles, bean sprouts, potatoes and *lento* in a serving bowl. Add 1–2 tablespoons black shrimp paste sauce. Pour hot soup over and garnish with fried shallots and garlic.

Opposite: (From top) Tahu Gimbal and Tahu Campur

Tahu Telur

(Bean Curd Fried in Eggs with Peanut Sauce)

5	eggs
1/2	teaspoon salt
1/4	teaspoon pepper
1	piece bean curd (8 x 8 cm), cut into 1/2 cm cubes, fried
100	grams bean sprouts, tailed, blanched, drained
1	teaspoon chopped Chinese parsley

Peanut Sauce (ground):

100	grams peanuts, fried
1	red chilli
5	bird's eye chillies
4	cloves garlic, sliced and fried
1/2	teaspoon salt and sugar to taste
2	tablespoons shrimp paste
2	tablespoons sweet soy sauce
1	teaspoon vinegar
50	cc water

Beat eggs with salt and pepper, then combine with bean curd. Mix thoroughly. Make a big omelette or two smaller ones. Set aside. ❧ Arrange omelette, bean sprouts and Chinese parsley on a serving dish. Add peanut sauce.

Peanut Sauce: Combine all the ingredients and mix well.

Tahu Isi

(Bean Curd Stuffed with Chicken and Shrimps)

6	pieces bean curd (7 x 7 cm), halved diagonally
100	grams minced chicken
75	grams minced shrimps
3	sprigs Chinese chives, sliced into 1 cm pieces
1/2	teaspoon salt
1/4	teaspoon pepper
1	egg, lightly beaten oil for deep-frying

Make a hole in each piece of bean curd so that filling can be added. Grind the bean curd pieces that have been dug out. ❧ Combine ground bean curd with minced chicken and shrimps, Chinese chives, salt, pepper and beaten egg. Mix well. ❧ Stuff the bean curd pieces with this filling until full. ❧ Deep-fry until golden brown. Drain and serve with sauce.

Sauce: Boil and grind 4 red chillies and 2 cloves garlic. Add 2–3 tablespoons sugar, 1 tablespoon vinegar and 50 cc water. Allow to simmer.

Note: Stuffed bean curd can also be steamed over low heat or boiled until they are floating. ❧ This dish can also be served as a soup. Add stuffed bean curds to 1250 cc stock, and add 2 sprigs chopped Chinese parsley, salt and pepper. Garnish with fried shallots.

Opposite: (From top) Tahu Isi and Tahu Telur

Tahu Berontak
(*Fried Stuffed Bean Curd*)
~

6	pieces bean curd (6 x 6 cm), halved diagonally
	oil for deep-frying

Filling:

2	tablespoons oil
100	grams minced shrimps
3	tablespoons carrots or yam beans, cut to the size of matchsticks
100	grams bean sprouts, tailed
1	tablespoon chopped Chinese parsley
2	tablespoons finely sliced spring onion

Spices (ground):

2	cloves garlic
3	shallots
1/2	teaspoon peppercorns
1/2	teaspoon salt

Dough:

100	grams rice flour
1	tablespoon cornstarch
125	cc water
3	cloves garlic, ground
1	teaspoon coriander, roasted and ground
3	candlenuts, ground
1	teaspoon chopped lesser galangal
1/2	teaspoon salt

Make a hole in each piece of bean curd so it can be stuffed.

Filling: With 2 tablespoons oil, sauté ground spices until fragrant. Add minced shrimps, carrots, bean sprouts, Chinese parsley and spring onion. Mix well and cook until soft. Set aside and let it cool. Stuff bean curd pieces with the filling.

Dough: Mix all the ingredients thoroughly. Dip stuffed bean curd pieces in the dough and deep-fry in hot oil until golden brown. Drain and serve.

Tahu Gejrot
(*Fried Bean Curd with Sweet-Sour Sauce*)
~

2	pieces large bean curd, quartered and fried
	fried shallots, for garnishing

Sauce:

100	grams brown sugar
250	cc water
4	shallots, ground
2	cloves garlic, ground
2	red chillies, ground
4	bird's eye chillies, ground
3–4	tablespoons sweet soy sauce
2	tablespoons tamarind juice

Prepare the sauce by first dissolving brown sugar in water. Add ground ingredients, sweet soy sauce and tamarind juice. Simmer over low heat until the mixture boils. ☙ Lightly mash fried bean curds and pour the sauce over it. Serve garnished with fried shallots.

Opposite: (From top) Tahu Berontak and Tahu Gejrot

EGGS

Telur Pindang
(Eggs Boiled with Herbs and Spices)

6	eggs
20	guava leaves, cleaned
2	*salam* leaves (or bay leaves as a substitute)
1	stalk lemon grass, bruised
1	tablespoon shallot skin
1	teaspoon chopped turmeric
1	slice galangal, bruised
1	tablespoon salt

Put eggs in a pan with the other ingredients, and cover with water. Boil for 10 minutes. ❧ Beat the shell lightly to crack them. Continue cooking over low heat for 1–2 hours until the colour and aroma are absorbed.

Note: Guava leaves add a reddish-brown tinge to the eggs; they can be substituted with 1 tablespoon tea leaves.

Sambal Goreng Telur
(Eggs in Spicy Coconut Milk)

3	tablespoons oil
3	shallots, finely sliced
1	*salam* leaf (or bay leaf as a substitute)
1	slice galangal, bruised
2	red chillies, sliced diagonally
150	grams medium-sized prawns, peeled
10	green beans (*petai*), halved
350	cc coconut milk from 1/2 coconut
1	tomato, chopped
6	eggs / 15 quail eggs, hard-boiled, peeled

Spices (ground):

3	red chillies
1/2	teaspoon chopped galangal
2	cloves garlic
4	shallots
	salt and brown sugar

Heat oil and sauté shallots. Add ground spices, *salam* leaf and galangal and fry until fragrant. Add chillies, prawns, *petai*, coconut milk and tomato. Allow to simmer. ❧ Add eggs and cook until the gravy thickens, stirring from time to time.

Note: It is easier to remove the shell if boiled eggs are first placed under cold running water and covered with cold water for a few minutes.

Martabak
(Indian Meat Pancake)

Dough:

200	grams wheat flour
1/2	teaspoon salt
50	grams oil / melted butter
3–4	tablespoons water

Filling:

1	tablespoon oil
1	clove garlic, minced
200	grams minced lamb / beef
1	teaspoon powdered coriander
1/4	teaspoon powdered cumin
1/8	teaspoon powdered aniseed
1/2	teaspoon pepper
1	teaspoon salt
1	small onion, minced
3–4	spring onions, finely sliced
1	sprig Chinese parsley, chopped
5–6	chicken or duck eggs, beaten

Dough: Combine flour and salt with 1 tablespoon oil and add water little by little. Knead gently into an oily, elastic dough. Make 6–7 balls. Place dough balls in a bowl and cover with the remaining oil. Let it stand for 1–6 hours. The dough will expand.

Filling: Heat oil and sauté garlic, minced meat, spices, pepper and salt. Stir well until mixture is fairly dry. Remove from heat and let it cool, then add onion, spring onions, Chinese parsley and eggs and mix well.

Making Martabak: With lightly oiled hands, pull out one ball of dough and flatten to make a large circle. Fry in a flat frying pan. Fill the centre of the dough with filling and fold in the sides. Fry until golden brown, then set aside. Do the same with the remaining dough. Serve with sauce.

Sauce: Bring to the boil 3 tablespoons vinegar. After it has cooled down, add 100 cc water, 4 tablespoons sweet soy sauce, 2 tablespoons chopped onions, 1 tablespoon sugar and a pinch of salt. Mix well.

Note: You can add curry powder to the filling.

Opposite: (Clockwise from top) Sambal Goreng Telur, Sambal Goreng Petis (page 188), Telur Pindang and Martabak

Sambal Goreng Petis
(Eggs in Black Shrimp Paste Sauce)

6	hard-boiled eggs
	oil for deep-frying
3	tablespoons oil
6	shallots, finely sliced
3	cloves garlic, finely sliced
1	*salam* leaf (or bay leaf as a substitute)
4	stalks lemon grass, finely sliced
2	slices young lesser ginger, peeled, finely sliced
8	tablespoons black shrimp paste
1	tablespoon fish paste
500	cc coconut milk
1	tablespoon tamarind juice
10	bird's eye chillies
	salt and brown sugar

Spices (ground):

1	tablespoon chopped young galangal
1	teaspoon chopped turmeric
1	teaspoon chopped ginger

Score the surface of the eggs and deep-fry until golden brown. Drain and set aside. ❦ Heat 3 tablespoons oil and sauté shallots and garlic until the colour changes. Add ground spices, *salam* leaf, lemon grass and lesser ginger, and fry until fragrant. ❦ Combine shrimp and fish paste with some coconut milk and add to the spices. Pour in the remaining coconut milk and bring to the boil. ❦ Add deep-fried eggs, tamarind juice, bird's eye chillies, salt and sugar. Continue to cook until the gravy thickens.

Note: Fish paste is used to moderate the colour and taste of the dish so that it is not too dark and not too sweet. It also makes the dish more tasty. This dish can be served with ketupat (compressed rice) or lontong (rice dumplings).

Sambal Plenet
(Mashed Eggs with Chilli Sauce)

4	hard-boiled eggs
4	red chillies
3	bird's eye chillies
2	teaspoons shrimp paste
1/2	teaspoon tamarind juice
1/2	teaspoon salt
	sugar
	basil leaves

Grind all the ingredients except basil leaves and eggs. ❦ Mash the eggs lightly, then pour ground spices over. Garnish with basil leaves.

Telur Balado
(Boiled Eggs in Chilli Sauce)

6	hard-boiled eggs
	oil for deep-frying
5	tablespoons oil
2	kaffir lime leaves, torn
1	tablespoon lime juice
1	tomato, chopped

Spices (ground):

10	red chillies
5	shallots
1	teaspoon salt

Score the surface of the eggs and deep-fry until golden brown. Set aside. ❦ Heat 5 tablespoons oil and sauté ground spices until soft, then add kaffir lime leaves, lime juice and tomato. Mix well, and add 1–2 tablespoons water if necessary. Continue to cook until the water is absorbed. ❦ Toss in the eggs and mix well.

Opposite: (From top) Sambal Plenet and Telur Balado

Orak-arik
(Scrambled Eggs with Mixed Vegetables)
~

3	tablespoons oil
3	cloves garlic, chopped
5	shallots, chopped
150	grams carrots, finely sliced
50	grams shrimps, chopped
3	cabbages, finely chopped
25	grams glass noodles, cut into 10 cm lengths, soaked in water until tender, drained
	salt
	pepper
3	eggs, lightly beaten

Heat oil and sauté garlic and shallots until golden brown. Add carrots and fry until they are tender. Add shrimps, cabbages, glass noodles and a pinch of salt and pepper. Mix well. ❧ Add lightly beaten eggs and keep stirring until it is mixed thoroughly with the vegetables. Remove from heat and serve.

Acar Tigu
(Pickled Eggs)
~

6	eggs, hard-boiled, peeled
	oil for deep-frying
3	tablespoons oil
3	red chillies, sliced into 1 cm pieces
3	green chillies, sliced into 1 cm pieces
100	cc water
1	tablespoon vinegar
1/2	teaspoon salt
1–2	tablespoons sugar

Spices (ground):

6	shallots
3	cloves garlic
1	teaspoon chopped ginger
1	teaspoon chopped turmeric

Score the surface of the eggs and deep-fry until golden brown. Drain and set aside. ❧ Heat 3 tablespoons oil and sauté ground spices until fragrant. Add chillies and stir until soft. Add water, vinegar, salt and sugar. Continue to cook until the sauce thickens.

Opposite: (From top) Orak-arik and Acar Tigu

Telur Tersembunyi

(Eggs Wrapped in Spiced Meat)
~

350	grams minced beef
2	slices bread, soaked in water, drained
1/2	teaspoon powdered nutmeg
1	teaspoon pepper
1/2	teaspoon salt
2	eggs, separate yolks and beat egg whites
5	eggs, hard-boiled, peeled, scored
	bread crumbs
	oil for deep-frying

Sauce:

1	tablespoon margarine
1	clove garlic, chopped
1	small onion, chopped
200	cc water / stock
3	tablespoons tomato sauce
1	tablespoon sweet soy sauce
	salt and pepper

Combine minced beef, bread, nutmeg, pepper, salt and egg yolks. Mix well and divide into 5 portions. ❧ Wrap each hard-boiled egg with one portion of the mixture. Dip it into egg white, and roll it over the bread crumbs. Dip into the egg white again, and roll over the bread crumbs once more. Deep-fry wrapped eggs until golden brown. Pour sauce over eggs and serve with fried potatoes and vegetables.

Sauce: Heat margarine and sauté garlic and onion until fragrant. Add stock and other ingredients. Cook until the sauce thickens.

Rendang Telur

(Eggs in Spicy Coconut Milk)
~

750	cc coconut milk from 2 coconuts
1/2	turmeric leaf, torn and knotted
5	kaffir lime leaves
2	stalks lemon grass, bruised
1–2	pieces dried sour fruit (*Garcinia cambogia*)
10	eggs / 30 quail eggs, hard-boiled, peeled

Spices (ground):

150	grams red chillies
3	cloves garlic
8	shallots
2	tablespoons chopped young galangal
2	teaspoons chopped ginger
2	teaspoons chopped turmeric
2	teaspoons powdered coriander

Bring to the boil coconut milk, ground spices, turmeric leaf, kaffir lime leaves and lemon grass. Add dried sour fruit and cook until the gravy thickens. ❧ Add the eggs, reduce heat and continue to cook. Stir from time to time until the gravy is golden brown and has thickened.

Intaluk Masak Habang

(Chilli Duck Eggs)
~

5	duck (or chicken) eggs, hard-boiled, peeled
1/2	teaspoon salt, mixed with 50 cc water
	oil for deep-frying
3	tablespoons oil
1–2	tomatoes, chopped
125	cc water
2–3	tablespoons sweet soy sauce

Spices (ground):

150	grams red chillies
3	cloves garlic
6	shallots
1/2	teaspoon dried shrimp paste
1	tablespoon sliced lemon grass
1	teaspoon chopped ginger
1	teaspoon chopped lesser galangal
	salt and brown sugar

Score the surface of the eggs and rub with salt water. Deep-fry eggs until golden brown, then set aside. ❧ Heat 3 tablespoons oil and sauté ground spices until fragrant. Add tomatoes, stir until soft, then pour in 125 cc water. Bring to the boil. ❧ Add sweet soy sauce and deep-fried eggs. Continue to cook until the sauce thickens.

Opposite: (Clockwise from top) Telur Tersembunyi, Rendang Telur and Intaluk Masak Habang

Botok Telur Asin

(Salted Eggs and Coconut in Banana Leaf)

~

125	cc thick coconut milk
6	teaspoons sliced shallots
1	teaspoon chopped garlic
3	red chillies, sliced diagonally
6	bird's eye chillies, sliced diagonally
	salt and sugar
12	slices galangal
6	*salam* leaves (or bay leaves as a substitute)
6	salted eggs, raw
25	grams basil leaves, coarsely chopped
	banana leaves

Combine coconut milk, shallots, garlic, chillies, salt and sugar. Mix thoroughly. ❧ Take 2 banana leaves, and add 2 slices galangal and 1 *salam* or bay leaf. Add 1 raw salted egg, 2–3 tablespoons spiced coconut milk and some chopped basil leaves. ❧ Fold leaves upwards and secure the top with toothpicks. Wrap other eggs in the same manner and steam for 30 minutes.

Pepes Telur

(Steamed Eggs in Banana Leaf)

~

10	eggs
1/2	teaspoon salt
1/4	teaspoon pepper
50	cc thick coconut milk
50	grams basil leaves
	banana leaves

Spices (ground):

10	red chillies
5	shallots
2	cloves garlic
1	tomato, chopped
3	candlenuts, roasted / fried
1	tablespoon chopped galangal
1	teaspoon chopped turmeric
1/2	teaspoon shrimp paste
2	teaspoons finely sliced lemon grass
	salt and sugar

Beat eggs lightly with salt and pepper, then steam in a bowl. Remove and let it cool. Cut into 1 cm cubes. ❧ Mix ground spices, coconut milk, basil leaves and cubed eggs. Divide into 10 portions. Wrap each portion in a banana leaf, roll up and secure both ends. ❧ Steam for 10 minutes. Remove from the steamer and grill over hot charcoal until dry.

Opposite: (From top) Pepes Telur and Botok Telur Asin

Dadar Isi
(Stuffed Omelette)
~

4	large eggs
4	tablespoons coconut milk
1/2	teaspoon salt
1/2	teaspoon powdered coriander
1/2	teaspoon pepper
	oil for frying omelettes

Filling:

2	tablespoons oil
1	*salam* leaf
200	grams minced beef
50	cc coconut milk
1	teaspoon wheat flour

Spices (ground):

2	red chillies
5	shallots
2	cloves garlic
1	*salam* leaf
1	teaspoon coriander
1	teaspoon chopped galangal

Filling: Sauté ground spices in 2 tablespoons oil until fragrant, then add *salam* leaf and minced beef. Stir until the ingredients are fairly dry, then pour in coconut milk. Continue to cook until the sauce is absorbed. Sprinkle flour and continue stirring until the mixture is well-combined and thoroughly cooked. Divide into 5–6 portions.

Omelette: Beat eggs with coconut milk, salt, coriander and pepper. Make 5–6 omelettes. On each omelette put a portion of the filling mixture, then roll up. Serve.

Dadar Gembung
(Duck Egg Omelette)
~

5	duck eggs
1	teaspoon salt
5	red chillies, ground
3	shallots, ground
3	tablespoons shredded coconut, ground
2–3	spring onions, finely sliced
1	sprig Chinese parsley, chopped
	oil for frying omelette

Beat eggs with salt and ground chillies and shallots. ❧ Add ground shredded coconut, spring onions and Chinese parsley, and mix well. ❧ Heat oil, pour in the egg mixture and cook in a covered pan for 2–3 minutes. Turn the omelette over carefully and fry until thoroughly cooked. Cut into serving pieces.

Opposite: (From left) Dadar Isi and Dadar Gembung

Index